THE SPIRIT

OF CRICKET

ROB SMYTH

WHAT MAKES CRICKET THE GREATEST
GAME ON EARTH

E&T

First published in 2010 by
Elliott and Thompson Ltd
27 John Street, London WC1N 2BX
www.eandtbooks.com

Paperback edition published in 2011
978-1-90764-220-3

Electronic edition published in 2011
978-1-90764-212-8

9 8 7 6 5 4 3 2 1

A CIP catalogue record for this book is available from
the British Library.

Printed in the UK by CPI Group

The contributions from Michael Brearley and Sir Richard Hadlee were first published by
The International Cricket Council.

Every effort has been made to trace copyright holders for extracts used within
this book. Where this has not been possible the publisher will be happy to credit
them in future editions.

ACKNOWLEDGMENTS

There are so many people who helped with this book – the majority of whom I have not even met, only admired as they went to work on a cricket field – that it is impossible to list them all. And I'm not only saying that to cover myself in the inevitable event of forgetting somebody important. I owe a particular debt of gratitude to Lorne Forsyth, Ellen Marshall, Cris Freddi, Scott Murray, Gary Naylor, Richard O'Hagan, Paul King, James Henderson and Adam Chadwick.

The contributors, amongst them some of the true greats of the game, were remarkably generous with their time: Richie Benaud, Dickie Bird, Sir Ian Botham, Michael Brearley, Andy Bull, Alan Davies, Duncan Fletcher, David Gower, Tony Greig, Sir Richard Hadlee, Michael Holding, Nasser Hussain, Mahela Jayawardene, Mitchell Johnson, Jacques Kallis, Robert Key, David Lloyd, Christopher Martin-Jenkins, Sam Mendes, Alison Mitchell, Eoin Morgan, Mark Nicholas, Ricky Ponting and Graeme Smith. It is purely coincidental that the list ends at S. I never did manage to track down Kapila Wijegunawardene.

I'd especially like to thank John English for his skilful editing, and Mark Searle for his advice and ceaseless patience, particularly every time the phone cut out while one of us was on a train. Finally I'd like to thank Dr Colin Butler for introducing me to the joy of words; Tim de Lisle for introducing me to the joy of writing; my father, John, for introducing me to the joy of sport; and my mother, Betty, for introducing me to the joy of life.

Rob Smyth is an experienced sports journalist who writes regularly for the *Guardian* and *Wisden*. He has also been published in *GQ Style*, *Intelligent Life* and *FourFourTwo*. He has a peculiarly rewarding obsession with Martin McCague.

INTRODUCTION

When television cameramen cut to the crowd during a sporting event, they invariably focus on three types: the beautiful, the famous and the wacky. Yet when those cameras lingered, apparently inexplicably, on a random middle-aged woman during the final Ashes Test of 2009, it provided a different and infinitely more rewarding type of beauty.

The woman was desperately biting her clenched fist in an attempt to stop herself from haemorrhaging tears. This was not, as might reasonably have been presumed, the default setting of the England cricket fan during an Ashes series, but the reaction of Donna Trott to the sight of her son, Jonathan, reaching a glorious century on his Test debut.

Her attempt was doomed to failure, and tears of pride soon flowed. It was an extraordinary moment: in the midst of a monumental contest, the overriding emotion was of the wonderful poignancy of a mother's love for her son. It was the feelgood shot of the summer. In the context of such a fiercely contested sporting encounter, it was as incongruous as a lullaby in a heavy-metal song.

And yet in a sense it wasn't incongruous at all. Cricket has always had the capacity to transcend sport and, in that moment, the spirit of cricket – and the spirit of life – was in the rudest health. There are inherent contradictions in our understanding of the spirit of cricket. How could there not be? To one person the spirit of cricket would be embracing it as part of a rounded, cultured existence, as C. L. R. James did with his famous quote 'What do they know of cricket who only cricket know?'; yet to another it might manifest itself in an all-consuming love of the sport.

Equally, in the current climate many will surmise that Twenty20 is against the true spirit of cricket, yet the issue is not a simple one. In its early guise it had an innocence and a celebration of the game itself over winning and losing that truly evoked cricket's Golden Age; a hit-and-giggle philosophy which, at some level, resonated with the distant past. Similarly, after the inaugural World Cup in 1975, the umpire Dickie Bird said that 'It had everything. Such great players, and a freshness in spirit and approach that is not possible now.'

To some the pervasion of statistics is against the spirit; yet even many of those who hold such a view could not fail to be charmed by the sight of a small boy scoring every ball diligently on an idyllic summer's day. We can be at peace with these contradictions: cricket is a game which allows one of us to say 'tomay-to' and the other to say 'tomah-to' without ever feeling the need to call the whole thing off.

That which contravenes the spirit of cricket to one will embody it to another. The us-against-the-world captaincy of Arjuna Ranatunga manifested itself in a number of on-field contretemps, but in doing so he significantly accelerated the development of a cricket nation that currently provides more exceptional talents than any other.

Even within the accepted parameters of sportsmanship, there are contradictions. As Duncan Fletcher says, why is claiming a catch on the bounce seen as inherently reprehensible whereas not walking is widely acknowledged as part of the game?

The inevitable influence of national characteristics also serves to undermine a homogenised definition of the spirit of cricket. The same is true of eras. Our understanding of the concept has inevitably evolved; it seems remarkable now, but at the start of the 20th century it was emphatically the case that Test cricket was seen as being against the spirit of the game, an ideal that was firmly associated with the blissful innocence of county and village cricket. The spirit of cricket changes insidiously and intangibly; it is as marvellously elusive as the meaning of life.

Consequently, the aim of this book is not so much to define the spirit of cricket as to celebrate the myriad things that make cricket at least a unique sport and at best a superior one. Ostensibly, such an endeavour involves a significant focus on displays of sportsmanship; yet the longer the concept marinated, the broader its flavour became. This is not to suggest that cricket is whiter than the whites the players sometimes wear. Far from it; wrong'uns exist outside the legspin fraternity. This is not something of which cricket needs to be ashamed; there is no area of life that can legitimately claim the moral high ground, or a ticket to utopia.

DUNCAN FLETCHER

The spirit of cricket has become far more complicated than it needs to be. To me it is quite simple: if you are doing something that you would not want a child to copy in a game on a school playing field, then you are breaking the spirit of cricket. It is a question of conduct and respect. You are allowed to question the umpire, for example, but how do you go about doing it?

You would not want to see three fielders charging up and attacking the umpire over a decision in a school match, so that is conduct which I would say was against the spirit. The Laws may allow you to do something, but there is still the question of how you do it. Take appeals: they can be done responsibly or irresponsibly. Would you want to see children get down on their knees and shout at the umpire? No. It's excessive, and against the spirit.

Some people have a very confused understanding of what the spirit of cricket is. Claiming a catch on the bounce, for example, is often seen as cheating. Well, yes, it is, but I don't see why a fielder claiming the catch and leaving it to the umpire to make a decision is any different from a batsman nicking a catch behind and not walking. Yet one is seen as cheating and the other is not. How about when a batsman runs in front of the ball to block a throw for a run out? That's obstructing the fielder. What about when the non-striker leaves the crease before the bowler has delivered the ball?

That is trying to steal a run. It is all cheating, but some of it seen to be 'in the spirit' and some of it isn't.

The spirit of cricket is not about whether a player is cheating or not; it is about how he conducts himself on and off the field, the respect with which he treats the game and the courtesy he shows the players and umpires.

Duncan Fletcher was England coach 1999–2007

The spirit of cricket is very much in the eye of the beholder. It might be nothing more than the glazed look in a grown man's eye as he stares lovingly at a little urn, as Andrew Strauss did at the Oval in 2009. For the purposes of this book, it might be defined simply as that which makes cricket special to the individual. A personal memory is of staying up until the small hours in the early nineties, despite having school the next day, to play just one more over on the dice game 'International Cricket' by Lambourne Games, and then excitably regaling stories of my Test Championship to bemused classmates the following day. Ramiz Raja's 212-ball 52 never sounded so exciting. They might have had active social lives and the ability to make eye contact with the opposite sex, but I knew who was winning.

There were many who did not understand cricket at all, a situation that endures. During the 2009 Ashes, a Danish friend sent me an email which began: 'To take your mind off that dreadful game you call cricket . . .' It is not his fault that his soul is doomed to leave this world unfulfilled. The fact that cricket is so alien to so many gives cricket the feel of our little secret, almost of a cult, yet one that is also widespread; a plain-Jane-super-brain whose beauty few others can see. It is one of so many things that are unique to this magnificently ludicrous sport we all cherish.

The voice of the reformer is often the most powerful, and cricket's zeal for purity in part stems from its tainted past. The phrase 'It's not cricket' was a marketing technique in response to a number of match-fixing scandals in the 19th century; it was done so skilfully that it has come to refer to anything in life which is immoral. That it exists at all is fairly remarkable; after all, it's hard to imagine the phrase 'It's not football', 'It's not rugby', or 'It's not synchronised swimming'. That it has achieved quite such ubiquity is incredible.

Not least because, at the time the phrase was infiltrating the consciousness, cricket was embodied by a man in Dr W. G. Grace whose moral compass was, to say the least, a little restless. His habit of putting the bails back on after being bowled and informing the opposition that 'they've come to see me bat, not you bowl' is legendary.

He has grown into something of an anti-hero. Geoffrey Moorhouse describes him as 'not only one of the outstanding mercenaries of all time, but one of the most conspicuous offenders against that spirit of cricket which became glorified during his era and which he was supposed to represent.' Against that, cricket would be unrecognisable were it not for Grace dragging it kicking and screaming towards becoming a spectator sport. Perhaps the best summary comes from Matthew Engel: 'He exists in our imagination halfway between a child's conception of God, and Edward VII as played by Timothy West.'

Nobody could deny his influence. On his 50th birthday, the MCC moved the Gentlemen v Players match – at that time almost as big an occasion as Christmas – so it could serve as a celebration.

Grace lorded over the game at a time when the spirit of cricket, in England at least, was almost exclusively associated with county and particularly club cricket. Evolution is invariably governed not by the good but the bad, with change more often than not resulting from the latter than the former, and moral panics in cricket are nothing new. As Richie Benaud said so shrewdly during his 2001 Spirit of Cricket Cowdrey Lecture: 'Over the years neither behaviour nor the play itself has changed so much as people seem to think.' A heartfelt complaint that a belief in the spirit of cricket is seen as old-fashioned would have seemed entirely logical in 2009; that very complaint appeared in the *Manchester Guardian* on 18 April 1909.

Around that period, Test matches were seen by many as both too long and, irony of ironies, little more than a device for making money. 'The elders of the cricket rather believe that the Test matches do no one any good except the Australians, and theirs is simply a financial good,' said a piece in the *Guardian* in 1908. 'It would be difficult to find a real cricketer who would speak out for

7

the Tests as in the slightest degree beneficial to cricket as a game. Primarily there is little conduct in them that breathes the real spirit of cricket.'

It was not a fleeting viewpoint. As late as 1935, in a report of the final day of the West Indies' series victory over England, *The Times* cricket correspondent wrote: 'With all due respect to those who have to make such important decisions in the duty of the propagation of cricket, is there not a little too much of this so-called "Test match cricket"?'

When 186 runs were scored on the third day of the final Test between Australia and England in 1928–29, the *Manchester Guardian* correspondent had had enough. 'This Melbourne game has now lasted three days, and we are not yet within sight of the halfway stage,' he wrote. 'Is there anything good to be said for this sort of cricket? Is it even cricket at all? . . . I shall be only too happy to sing the praises of the modern Test match once its virtues are revealed to me.'

Another reason for the hostility towards Test cricket was what that same report described as 'the false sanctity of averages'. This was a recurring theme as the sport's Golden Age gave way to one of cold practice, when cricket hit a wall – or a Wall Street of emotionless achievement. In the 1909 *Wisden Cricketers' Almanack*, Alfred Lubbock wrote: 'I do not think the game (unless Gilbert Jessop is in and scoring) is quite so attractive as it was in the [eighteen] sixties.' The same year, the *Guardian*'s imperious dissection of a game newly obsessed with averages blamed 'bad bringing up' and 'being reared on a species of figure food', before concluding disgustedly that 'it would seem far more important for Tom Hayward to beat Mr Fry's aggregate of runs than that Surrey could beat Yorkshire'.

When Jack Hobbs famously passed W. G. Grace's record of 126 first-class centuries in 1925, there were some murmurs as to the relevance of such quantitative achievement. It was a perception that most had little truck with. 'We should indeed be surprised to hear anyone at the Kennington Oval lay an indictment against the great batsman,' noted the *Guardian*. 'After all, the scoring of centuries is certainly good cricket. I should be very much surprised if his captain, Mr [Percy] Fender, had any knowledge that Hobbs has ever overstepped the bounds not only of the Laws of the game, but ever in his life contravened the spirit of the game.'

The operative word was 'game'. An endearingly recurring phrase was simply 'the game's the thing'. For Hobbs, the game was the only thing. Yet even the virtuous nature of English cricket's most famous batsman could not reduce discontent with the development of county cricket. 'A blight has descended on championship cricket of the North of England,' wrote Cricketer in the *Guardian* in the 1927. 'Day after day the same dull tale has to be told. A team wins the toss, bats first on an easy wicket, lays a solid foundation for the innings, and then goes on the day long pushing and poking, risking nothing, making a wicked travesty of the best of games. The age of chivalry is gone; that of sophisters, economists and calculators has succeeded.'

The real spirit, many felt, was confined to the village green. 'In villages cricket is played for the game alone,' said the *Guardian* in

1926. '"Gates" are unimportant . . . and there is no time and less inclination for the pampering of players.' Even the public school match at Lord's the same year was subject to much criticism when it ended in a draw: 'a finish there ought to have been,' said *The Times*, 'if the true spirit of cricket shown by two very keen and level sides is to count for anything.'

For all that, facilitating a result through declaration – orthodox, not the contrivances that would come later – was not originally seen as acceptable. Until 1889 sides had to bat on until the last wicket fell, a situation that engendered umpteen farces. The most notable came during a match between Surrey and Sussex in 1887. Surrey, with a substantial lead, wanted to have a go at Sussex in the fourth innings; Sussex were equally keen to stay in the field. Thomas Bowley tried to get himself stumped, but the Sussex wicketkeeper declined to do so. Then Sussex bowled a number of no-balls to prolong the innings. By the time Bowley kicked his own stumps down, the damage was done: Sussex had taken enough time out of the game and escaped with a draw. When Surrey almost caused a minor riot by deliberately giving wickets away at Trent Bridge in a similar situation later that summer, the time had come for action and the law was soon changed.

Yet all these other problems paled in comparison to probably the biggest crisis cricket has known: Bodyline, the mother and father of all sporting international incidents that changed the game irrevocably.

BODYLINE

Victory rarely comes without some sort of price, but few have been as potentially great as during the Bodyline series in 1932–33. It was the series in which, as Michael Brearley put it, 'England won the Ashes and almost lost an empire.' You know a sporting contest is of serious importance when it has its own page on Wikipedia, eBay and even the Internet Movie Database. Bodyline is the only major cricket event to have been re-created on film.

The genre of that film was as much politics as sport. And the tagline was 'The day England declared war on Australia'. There is so much to say about Bodyline that it could fill an entire book of its own. Of the many books it has spawned, David Frith's majestic *Bodyline Autopsy* stands out as a definitive work.

For the uninitiated, Bodyline was a response to the superhuman talent of Don Bradman, who had scored 974 runs in the 1930 Ashes series. It came about when England's cold, unyielding captain, Douglas Jardine, had his own 'Eureka!' moment, announcing: 'I've got it: he's yellow,' after studying footage of Bradman flinching on a lively wicket at The Oval in 1930. The tactic involved bowling at the body with a cradle of close-in fielders on the leg side. It made run-scoring a hugely risky enterprise in terms of preserving one's wicket and even one's life.

In statistical terms it was an unmitigated triumph: England won 4–1 – their only victory in an Ashes series between 1928 and 1953 – and Bradman's series average was 56.57, well down on his career average of 99.94. Yet there was so much more to it than that. The dangerous nature of England's approach was the real issue. Bert Oldfield fractured his skull when he missed a pull at Harold Larwood (although Larwood was bowling to a conventional field at the time); the Australian captain Bill Woodfull collapsed after taking a sickening blow on the heart, at which point Jardine pointedly shouted: 'Well bowled, Harold', largely for the benefit of Bradman at the non-striker's end.

Relations between England and Australia broke down almost completely. When Woodfull, who refused publicly to complain or copy England's tactics, received a visit from the England manager Pelham Warner in the dressing-room at Adelaide, he famously said, 'There are two teams out there. One is trying to play cricket and the other is not', a line which, to his chagrin, was soon leaked.

There were fears of a riot during the third Test at Adelaide, with mounted police gathered outside the ground, although it never materialised. *Wisden* described that match as 'probably the most unpleasant Test ever played', and asserted that 'the whole atmosphere was a disgrace to cricket'.

During that match, the Australian Cricket Board sent a telegram to England which threatened relations between the countries. 'Bodyline bowling has assumed such proportions as to menace the best interests of the game, making protection of the body by the batsmen the main consideration. This is causing intensely bitter feeling between the players as well as injury. In our opinion it is unsportsmanlike. Unless stopped at once it is likely to upset the friendly relations existing between Australia and England.'

The MCC, not realising the severity of the situation, responded brusquely. 'We . . . deplore your cable . . . We have fullest confidence in captain, team and managers and are convinced that they would do nothing to infringe either the Laws of Cricket or the spirit of the game . . . if it is such as to jeopardise the good relations between English and Australian cricketers and you consider it desirable to cancel remainder of programme we would consent, but with great reluctance.'

The matter was raised in Cabinet but, after much to-ing and fro-ing, the ACB backed down a little, conscious of the financial implications of a complete meltdown. Not that it ended with the series: the MCC decided to wash their hands of Bodyline and ordered Larwood to sign a written apology. When he refused, feeling he was being made a scapegoat, he was blackballed. Despite being 28 and the best fast bowler in the world, he never played for his country again.

The Laws would inevitably be changed with regard to short-pitched bowling and leg-side fields, although Bodyline remains cricket's signature crisis. As much as anything, it accentuated the distinction between the Laws and the spirit, and rammed home the need to play within both.

Despite that, and the general acceptance that England's tactics compromised the spirit of the game, attitudes towards the series and its protagonists have evolved significantly. 'This mellowing reflects not merely the passage of time but the changing of fashion,' wrote Gideon Haigh, the game's premier historian. 'Batsmen skewered by pace from four prongs in the 1970s and 1980s found it hard to imagine bowling any more hostile; and if they could take it, then could Bodyline *really* have been so bad?'

Bodyline was far from a simple case of good versus evil, right versus wrong, Australia versus England. Was Jardine the man who, John Arlott said, 'among Australians, is probably the most disliked of cricketers', or a man whose tactical ingenuity and emphasis on looking after his team to the exclusion of everything else would later be repeated by the likes of Arjuna Ranatunga? 'To me and every member of the 1932–33 MCC side in Australia, Douglas Jardine was the greatest captain England ever had,' said Bill Bowes. 'A great fighter, a grand friend, and an unforgiving enemy.'

His opposite number, Bill Woodfull, was the good guy of Bodyline, but even his role has been questioned. 'This stoical acceptance of England's strategy for the sake of imperial harmony has a certain nobility, but it is also strangely lacking in imagination,' wrote Gideon Haigh in 2007. 'It left Woodfull's comrades to solve by their own lights the perplexities Bodyline posed.'

Finally Larwood, who vividly recalled a child saying 'Mummy, he doesn't look like a murderer' during the series, would become an adopted son of Australia, emigrating there on the suggestion of Jack Fingleton, who had opened the Australian batting in three of the Bodyline Tests.

Australia were involved in another significant incident in 1947–48, when the Indian all-rounder Vinoo Mankad ran Bill Brown out for backing up too far. The practice, within the letter of the Laws but firmly against the spirit, became known as 'Mankading'. For decades it was left to the individual's conscience – Kapil Dev did the same to South Africa's Peter Kirsten as recently as 1992–93 – but the law was eventually changed so that a bowler could not run a batsman out once he had started his delivery stride.

The other major cricket controversy of the 20th century, described by Richie Benaud as 'disgraceful . . . one of the worst things I have ever seen on a cricket field', was Trevor Chappell's underarm delivery against New Zealand in 1981. With the New Zealand number 10 Bruce McKechnie needing to hit a six from the final ball of the match, his first, just to tie the third World Series final at Melbourne, Greg Chappell instructed his brother Trevor to roll an underarm delivery along the ground so that McKechnie could not hit a six. It caused an almighty storm – the New Zealand prime minister Robert Muldoon said that it was apt Australia were playing in yellow – and prompted an inevitable law-change.

If that was a risible exploitation of the rules, then slightly more imaginative manipulations of the Laws have also been deemed against the spirit over the course of time. In 1979, the Middlesex captain Mike Brearley, keen to enliven a dying match against Yorkshire, put a helmet at midwicket when the left-arm spinner Phil Edmonds was bowling; the logic being that, if the Yorkshire batsmen tried to get five runs by hitting the helmet, they would have to play riskily against the spin. The Laws were soon revised with a section on where the helmet could and could not be placed.

In 1996, another captain with a wonderfully keen mind, Warwickshire's Dermot Reeve, was batting to save a match on the final day against Hampshire, and particularly their left-arm spinner Raj Maru. With Maru bowling into the rough outside leg stump, Reeve started to throw his bat away so that, if he was caught off the glove, he could not be given out. It was fiendish and ingenious; it was also soon outlawed.

Such incidents led to the perception that the spirit of cricket was being eroded, which in turn led to Ted Dexter and Colin Cowdrey suggesting a formal Preamble to the Laws of the game. 'He [Dexter] hugely admired the way in which golf was self-regulated by players who knew the game was not only bigger than they were,' said his son Jeremy, 'but had very special values that had to be preciously guarded.' The Preamble was announced in 1999 and introduced in 2000.

THE SPIRIT OF CRICKET PREAMBLE

Cricket is a game that owes much of its unique appeal to the fact that it should be played not only within its Laws but also within the Spirit of the Game. Any action which is seen to abuse this spirit causes injury to the game itself. The major responsibility for ensuring the spirit of fair play rests with the captains.

1. There are two Laws which place responsibility for the team's conduct firmly on the captain.

Responsibility of captains

The captains are responsible at all times for ensuring that play is conducted within the Spirit of the Game as well as within the Laws.

Player's conduct

In the event of a player failing to comply with instructions by an umpire, or criticising by word or action the decision of an umpire, or showing dissent, or generally behaving in a manner which might bring the game into disrepute, the umpire concerned shall in the first place report the matter to the other umpire and to the player's captain, and instruct the latter to take action.

2. Fair and unfair play

According to the Laws the umpires are the sole judges of fair and unfair play.

The umpires may intervene at any time and it is the responsibility of the captain to take action where required.

3. The umpires are authorised to intervene in cases of:

Time wasting

Damaging the pitch

Dangerous or unfair bowling

Tampering with the ball

Any other action that they consider to be unfair

4. The Spirit of the Game involves RESPECT for:

Your opponents

Your own captain

The roles of the umpires

The game's traditional values

5. **It is against the Spirit of the Game:**

   To dispute an umpire's decision by word, action or gesture

   To direct abusive language towards an opponent or umpire

   To indulge in cheating or any sharp practice, for instance:

   (a) to appeal knowing that the batsman is not out

   (b) to advance towards an umpire in an aggressive manner when appealing

   (c) to seek to distract an opponent either verbally or by harassment with persistent clapping or unnecessary noise under the guise of enthusiasm and motivation of one's own side

6. **Violence**

   There is no place for any act of violence on the field of play.

7. **Players**

   Captains and umpires together set the tone for the conduct of a cricket match. Every player is expected to make an important contribution towards this.

The consequence was a significantly heightened awareness of the concept, aided also by the introduction of the Spirit of Cricket Cowdrey Lecture, which has taken place at the start of every English summer from 2001. The inaugural speaker was Richie Benaud, who has been succeeded in order by Barry Richards, Sunil Gavaskar, Clive Lloyd, Geoffrey Boycott, Martin Crowe,

Christopher Martin-Jenkins, The Most Reverend Dr Desmond Tutu, Adam Gilchrist and Imran Khan.

The introduction of match referees in 1993 was also partly designed to protect the spirit of cricket. But if cricket is to reflect the good in life, it must also reflect the bad, and there have been all manner of incidents in the last 20 years. During a particularly fractious Test between Sri Lanka and England in Kandy in 2001, one that *Wisden* described as a 'bar-room brawl', the former Hampshire captain Mark Nicholas, writing in the *Daily Telegraph*, said: 'Every player should have to recite "The Spirit of Cricket" until he is blue in the face otherwise we will all go blue in the face watching them turn this most special game into a joke.'

Two winters later, when Michael Vaughan made a thrilling 177 against Australia at Adelaide only after he survived Justin Langer's claims for a low catch early on, the *Australian* newspaper pronounced the spirit of cricket dead.

On a day when England's troubled tour came to life through a wonderful Michael Vaughan century, the spirit of cricket was pronounced dead by the actions of the players. [The game's spirit] clearly is now irrelevant in this uncompromising, unforgiving, graceless age of professionalism. Batsmen are entitled to wait for the umpire to give them out even if they appear clearly caught. Bowlers are entitled to appeal even if the crowd feel the ball has bounced. This is what happened yesterday and cricket is poorer for it.

And yet, and yet. For all the inevitable controversies, there have been, as we shall see, so many wonderful examples of the spirit of cricket in the last decade. The very fact that it is so widely discussed suggests a game which, if not in rude health, is at least conscious of its responsibilities. During the Ashes and the Champions Trophy in 2009, you could scarcely move for debates about what was and was not in the spirit of the game.

The ICC has continued to push the concept. The 2006 Champions Trophy was dedicated to the Spirit of Cricket, while a year earlier Getty Images produced a Spirit of Cricket exhibition. The ICC also released its own book, *The Spirit of Cricket*, full of compelling imagery of the game's history. And in 2009 it launched the Catch The Spirit initiative as part of its centenary celebrations.

In the Autumn of 2009, *The Times* carried an extended debate as to what the spirit of cricket was and whether it even existed. It involved three generations of their cricket correspondents, John Woodcock, Christopher Martin-Jenkins and Mike Atherton, as well as their chief sports writer Simon Barnes. The spirit of cricket is very much a live topic, one that has changed throughout 150 years and will continue to do so. We cannot be sure what direction it will take, but we can probably be sure that Donna Trott will not be the last mother reduced to tears of joy by this most human of games.

CHAPTER ONE

A predilection for using the nearest mirror may ostensibly be the preserve of the self-centred, but it can signify virtue rather than vanity. The desire for constant self-inspection, to be true to thine own self, is surely the essence of the spirit of cricket. During his time as England coach, Duncan Fletcher gave every England player a copy of Dale Wimbrow's poem 'The Guy In The Glass' ('Your final reward will be heartache and tears/If you've cheated the guy in the glass') and was even asked to read it out on BBC Radio.

For the most part, the obligation on cricketers to take the appropriate degree of personal responsibility is not so formally expressed. A culture of doing the right thing has evolved over centuries. That evolution has taken it into unexpected areas. Forty years ago, when 'walking' – a batsman accepting his dismissal and returning to the pavilion without waiting for the umpire's verdict – was an almost universal practice, it would have been unthinkable that the landscape could change to such an extent that walking would become one of the cornerstones of contemporary discussions of the spirit of cricket.

The former England batsman and coach David Lloyd says that, in the early seventies, there were only three batsmen in county cricket who did not walk – and that everyone knew who they were. Similarly, the young Lancashire side of which Lloyd was such a key part were told that if they did not walk, they did not play. If it wasn't quite a given that a batsman walked when he had hit the ball – there were sporadic controversies, even in the Golden Age – then it was strongly ingrained.

Cultures invariably change imperceptibly, and there was no single incident that symbolised the newfound inclination of batsmen to stand their ground and take their chances with the umpire's decision. But there was certainly one moment that came to represent walking as an issue in the modern game: Adam Gilchrist's decision to give himself out against Sri Lanka in 2003.

ADAM GILCHRIST
AUSTRALIA V SRI LANKA, WORLD CUP SEMI-FINAL, PORT ELIZABETH, 18 MARCH 2003

The notion of voices in the head has connotations of something dark and sinister, but the opposite was true during the incident that changed Adam Gilchrist's life in 2003. He had got Australia off to a flyer in their World Cup semi-final against Sri Lanka when he inside-edged a sweep at Aravinda de Silva onto his pads, from where it looped into the gloves of the wicketkeeper Kumar Sangakkara. As Gilchrist rose to his feet to walk off, the umpire Rudi Koertzen gave him not out. Any temptation Gilchrist might have had to stand his ground lasted no longer than a millisecond. 'The voice in my head was emphatic. Go. Walk. And I did.'

His decision captured the imagination in a way that no other example of a batsman walking has done; partly because it was such a high-profile game and especially because Gilchrist is an Australian, a breed who, as the joke goes, only walk when their car runs out of petrol/they miss the bus/the scales break and they have an epiphany.

Ultimately his action was scarcely more or less worthy than any of the times he has walked, or any of the myriad occasions on which other modern players like Brian Lara and Kumar Sangakkara have done so. Lara, for example, walked when nine shy of a century in the third Test against India at Mohali in 1994–95.

Gilchrist's greatest contribution to the game was arguably not to walk but to discuss it openly: seen by some as self-serving, in reality he displayed a hugely courageous willingness to further the good of the game even though he risked being ostracised both by opponents (New Zealand captain Stephen Fleming accused him of being on a 'crusade') and his own team (Gilchrist said that, in the few hours after he walked against Sri Lanka, he felt 'more lonely than I had ever felt among a cricket team' and 'silently accused of betraying the team').

Whether that was the case or not, the judgement from afar was much more generous. *Wisden Cricketers' Almanack* called it simply 'Gilchrist's match'. Gilchrist put walking, an apparently antiquated concept, back on the agenda for discussion. By delving into a more chivalrous past, he was years ahead of his time.

Australia (212-7) beat Sri Lanka 123-7 by 38 runs (Duckworth/Lewis method)

Walking takes more courage than we realise. The good Samaritan runs the risk of being labelled a goody two shoes. Steve James, the *Daily Telegraph* cricket writer who played two Tests for England in 1998, walked in two of his four innings. In a parallel universe, James the non-walker might have played 30 Tests. 'They were instinctive reactions,' he said, 'and despite some mutterings in the England dressing room, I was glad skipper Alec Stewart silenced them with: "That's the way he plays, so that should be it."'

Yet even Adam Gilchrist has not always walked. His moral compass changed direction irrevocably because of the guilt he felt after declining to walk during a 2nd XI game for New South Wales. Gilchrist went on to make a hundred, but the guilt nagged at him. 'I felt so bad afterwards that I went to apologise to the bowler, who was a 38-year-old veteran. He said, "Don't worry, this game obviously means more to you than it does to me." And I thought, "Yeah, but still. At what cost?"' Gilchrist vowed never to stand his ground again if he knew he had hit the ball.

Has Gilchrist ever declined to walk since? Probably only he knows, but the fact that, in a world that revels in exposing imperfections, no specific incident has been cited is strongly in his favour. Either way, judgements of walking can never be black-and-white. Some felt that Colin Cowdrey was a selective walker, while

Gilchrist says that, during a chat with Brian Lara about the subject, Lara admitted that he only walked if he was pretty sure the umpire had heard a nick. During a contretemps over a low catch in the Leeds Test of 1966, Basil D'Oliveira suggested that Garry Sobers, one of cricket's renowned walkers, had twice failed to do so in a Lancashire League match a few years earlier. This is not to decry Cowdrey, Lara or Sobers, who would figure with varying degrees of prominence in any discussion of players who encapsulate the spirit of cricket. When it comes to walking, there is no Venn diagram, just a state of flux in which individual approaches are always open to change.

Generally walking is seen as a straightforward moral issue, but occasionally it has been done with simple human consideration for another. At Adelaide in 1950–51, the Australian captain Ian Johnston walked to give England's hapless medium-pacer John Warr his first and only Test wicket on the way to a bowling average of 281, the worst in England's Test history. (Although Ravi Bopara had moved stealthily to 199 by the time he was dropped during the 2009 Ashes.) Walking also has an obvious benefit for umpires. When Tatenda Taibu gave himself out in 2003, the late David Shepherd said, 'Well walked, young man.'

As Tony Greig says, the game previously had a foolproof referral system for edges and catches: the word of the players. A happy side-effect of the Umpire Decision Referral System might be an increase in walking, given the apparent futility of standing your ground if there is sufficient technology to confirm an edge one way or another.

Moral dilemmas are equally acute when it comes to bowlers or fielders claiming dubious wickets. Broadly such instances fall into two categories: catches where the ball has bounced just in front of the fielder, or dismissals that are within the Laws but not the spirit. The latter was particularly evident during the Champions Trophy in 2009. First the England captain Andrew Strauss withdrew an appeal for the run-out of Sri Lanka's Angelo Mathews after he collided mid-pitch with Graham Onions; then the New Zealand captain Daniel Vettori did likewise when Paul Collingwood was run out, having absent-mindedly left his crease before the umpire signalled the end of the over.

EOIN MORGAN

An incident that summed up the spirit of cricket to me occurred during last year's Champions Trophy match between England and New Zealand. I was at the non-striker's end when Paul Collingwood came down the pitch to do a bit of gardening before the umpire had called 'over', and Brendon McCullum ran him out. Technically he should have been out, but the New Zealand captain Daniel Vettori withdrew the appeal because, while it was right by the Laws of cricket, it was against the spirit.

It all seemed to happen really quickly: one minute I thought he was out, which would have put us in real trouble, and the next it was over. It was quite funny really because of what had happened the previous year, when Colly was captain and there was controversy over the run-out of a New Zealand player, Grant Elliott.

Obviously there's a rich tradition of these things in cricket; there's a great spirit that holds it all together. You don't get massive cheating, things like diving in football. I wouldn't say I was taught about the spirit of the game as a youngster. You just pick it up through watching how other people conduct themselves. I think it helps that cricket is not an erratic sport: the structure gives people time to think about what is the right thing to do. It's a cooler, calmer game than most others.

Eoin Morgan, England 2008–

It is easy to surmise that there is simply a right and a wrong, and that of course players should not claim undeserved wickets. But it is not easy to find the strength to do so when a match, or even a career, is in the balance. Courtney Walsh left the Lahore pitch in tears in 1987 after his last over went for 14, giving Pakistan a crucial World Cup victory by one wicket. Before the final over Walsh, with figures of 9-1-26-4, was the likely Man of the Match. Instead he was remembered as the man who cost West Indies the game and, ultimately, a place in the semi-finals for the first time in a World Cup. On reflection, his decision not to run out Saleem Jaffar for backing up too far ahead of the final delivery put far more credit in the bank than the defeat took out.

MICHAEL HOLDING

One incident I remember vividly, even though I wasn't playing, involved Courtney Walsh against Pakistan in Lahore during the 1987 World Cup. Pakistan needed two off the last ball to win with their last pair at the crease. The non-striker Saleem Jaffar had been constantly backing up too far and he was well out of his crease for the final ball, but instead of running him out Courtney just told him, 'Don't do that' and went back to his mark. West Indies lost when Abdul Qadir hit the last ball for two.

Courtney was always very magnanimous, and his behaviour far exceeds anything that I've seen from people who have been put in that position. I certainly wouldn't have taken it the way he did. Normally you give a batsman a first warning, that is the procedure, but it wasn't the first time Jaffar had done it and it was such an important game, so he would have been entitled to say: 'Enough of this, out you go.' And as it turned out, had West Indies won that game they would have reached the semi-final instead of Pakistan.

Michael Holding, West Indies 1975–87

Courtney Walsh played 132 Tests and 205 ODIs for the West Indies, taking a total of 746 wickets

A sibling of Walsh's effort also came against Pakistan, at Multan in 2003. With Bangladesh within two wickets of their inaugural Test victory, Mohammad Rafique declined to run out Umar Gul for backing up too far. Gul added 52 for the ninth wicket with Inzamam-ul-Haq, who guided Pakistan to victory by one wicket. There have been equally famous examples of fielders recalling batsmen who have wrongly been given out: Rod Marsh's decision to call back Derek Randall almost cost Australia the Centenary Test of 1977; Gundappa Viswanath doing likewise to Bob Taylor did cost India the Jubilee Test of 1979–80, when Taylor batted for nearly five hours and took part in a match-winning partnership of 171 with Ian Botham. 'I don't regret recalling Bob Taylor,' said Viswanath later. 'I guess some people didn't like it but it doesn't worry me. I'm happy that I called him back. It was simple. He wasn't out.'

ROD MARSH
AUSTRALIA V ENGLAND, CENTENARY TEST, MELBOURNE, 12–17 MARCH 1977

Perhaps no single Test match has embodied the spirit of cricket more than the Centenary Test of 1977. *Wisden* said that Hans Ebeling, the former Australian Test bowler whose idea it was, 'should have been christened Hans Andersen Ebeling'. It was a sensational cricket match but, more importantly, a near-perfect cricket occasion.

There was so much to warm hearts and minds. A fascinatingly unusual narrative, with the first innings producing 233 runs and the second 836; the delightful coincidence of Australia's victory margin of 45 runs, exactly the same as in the very first Test match 100 years earlier; the courage of Rick McCosker, coming out to bat at number 10 with a broken jaw – his was the only jaw that didn't drop when he emerged from the pavilion – and holding out while 54 ultimately decisive runs were scored; the presence at the match of 218 of the 244 living cricketers to have played in the Ashes, with the 84-year-old Percy Fender flying over from Britain despite being nearly blind; the tragically unfulfilled promise of David Hookes, who struck Tony Greig for five consecutive fours on his Test debut; and the mischievous brilliance of Derek Randall's 174, a performance that Michael Barrett in *Observer Sport Monthly* described as 'English cricket's defining innings – brave, eccentric, obdurate and charming'.

It was during Randall's knock that perhaps the signature moment of the game occurred. He was on 161, with England just past 300 for the loss of four wickets in pursuit of 463, when he fiddled outside off stump at Max Walker and was given out caught behind. But as he trudged off to the pavilion, Rod Marsh informed the umpire and his captain Greg Chappell that he could not be sure the ball had carried.

Despite the obvious importance of the wicket, Chappell instantly called Randall back. 'Would that this spirit was always so!' said the *Wisden* match report. In the end, it did not matter; Randall added 13 more before he was caught off Kerry O'Keeffe, and Australia squeaked home. Chappell and Marsh were not to know that, of course, and despite the remorseless desire for victory of perhaps the most macho team in cricket history, they did not lose sight of more important values. 'That was fantastic,' said Dennis Lillee, 'and shows no matter how hard we played, we played fair.'

Two weeks later Chappell received a letter from Walter Hadlee, the father of Sir Richard and President of the New Zealand Cricket Association, commending both him and Marsh. 'Neither you nor Rod will have any regrets,' he wrote, 'for you have placed the game above winning.' It was a fitting legacy of a game that, more than most Test matches, was about so much more than winning and losing. As Henry Blofeld wrote in the *Guardian*: 'The year 2077 will have something to live up to.'

Australia (138 & 419-9 dec) beat England (95 & 417) by 45 runs

Another Indian captain, Kapil Dev, cost his side a World Cup group match against Australia at Chennai in 1987 by agreeing with Australia's submission that a Dean Jones stroke off Maninder Singh – originally signalled as four – had gone for six. Australia won by one run. On other occasions, acts of chivalry have had no impact whatsoever. At Lord's in 1997 Ian Healy said he wasn't sure whether an edge from Graham Thorpe had carried, an act for which he was pointedly applauded by the umpire David Shepherd. It didn't matter, as Glenn McGrath routed England for 77. Healy would not have known this, of course, and only the most intractable cynic would accuse players of selectivity in this area.

CHRISTOPHER MARTIN-JENKINS

I think it is important not to be too idealistic about the spirit of cricket which, as any player knows, is a tough game. But it is also a game that can be ruined by garrulous behaviour or downright sharp practice.

Cricketers of any nationality seem to know as much by instinct as upbringing when something is wrong and against the spirit, such as someone appealing when he (or she) knows perfectly well it is not out, or when a batsman fails to walk even when he knows for certain that he has been fairly caught. The onus is on captains, who should encourage a generous approach to any game but always in the context of trying to win by fair means. The worse the umpires, the greater the need for players not to try to take advantage by unfair means.

On the other hand the greater the stakes, the more acts of generosity are appreciated by everyone. The sight of Andrew Flintoff's heartfelt condolences to Brett Lee after the desperately narrow England win at Edgbaston in 2005 is fresh in the memory but the most remarkable example of the proper spirit which I can recall was the one given by Australia's wicketkeeper, Wally Grout, on the first morning of the 1964 Ashes series at Trent Bridge.

Fred Titmus, opening the batting because John Edrich had turned an ankle by treading on a ball in practice (there's nothing new under the sun) was knocked over accidentally by Neil Hawke as he attempted a quick single in response to a call from Geoff Boycott, whose first Test innings it was. Grout could have run Titmus out by yards but declined to do so. What a way to set the tone for a series and what an example to lesser players at all levels.

Christopher Martin-Jenkins MBE has been cricket correspondent of the BBC (1973–80 and 1985–91), the Daily Telegraph *(1990–99) and the* Times *(1999–2008)*

Wally Grout played 51 Tests for Australia from 1957 to 1966, claiming 187 dismissals. Fred Titmus played 53 Tests for England from 1955 to 1975, scoring 1,449 runs at 22.29 and taking 153 wickets at 32.22

Abstinence can also be seen in areas of potential controversy such as sledging and short-pitched bowling. Gubby Allen was famously opposed to England's Bodyline tactics in 1932–33, in which he sometimes shared the new ball with Harold Larwood, and in the seventies and eighties the Test-playing nations agreed an amnesty on bouncing tailenders, with each side allotted a certain number of lower-order players who would be exempt from short-pitched bowling. The development was described as 'namby-pambyness' by Mike Brearley, a man who many might, perhaps a little simplistically, have expected to support it.

An individual's comprehension of the spirit of cricket is inevitably shaped by their upbringing. Dynasties have coursed through the history books from the start: a list of the most famous includes the Graces, the Cowdreys, the Pollocks, the Mohammads, the Headleys, the Amarnaths and the Chappells (whose grandfather, Vic Richardson, played 19 Tests between 1924 and 1936, including all five in the Bodyline series of 1932–33).

Over 100 families have produced related Test players, while two have straddled three generations: the Headleys (George and Ron of the West Indies; Dean of England) and the Khans of Pakistan (Jahangir, the great Majid, and Bazid). Some Tests have doubled up as family meetings. At The Oval in 1880, the three Grace brothers played for England against Australia. Similarly, Hanif, Mushtaq and Sadiq Mohammad all played for Pakistan against New Zealand at Karachi in 1969–70.

And at Harare in 1997–98, three sets of brothers – Andy and Grant Flower, John and Gavin Rennie, and Paul and Bryan Strang – played for Zimbabwe against New Zealand. Their experiences have not always been joyous: when Mark Waugh was picked for his Test debut against England in 1990–91 it was at the expense of his twin Steve (although they would go on to play a record 108 Tests together); the ripped genes of Jeff and Simon Jones, father and son, meant a succession of injuries that restricted them to 15 and 18 (not out) Tests respectively.

Whether as part of a dynasty or not, family life has offered an almost infinite selection of moments that encapsulate a love of cricket. It might be incessant cricket chatter around the Benaud dinner table; Stuart Broad bouncing on Courtney Walsh's lap as a child; A. B. de Villiers fielding for hours and hours in the backyard until he was permitted a bat by his older brothers, and then playing so well that they soon tried to knock his head off. You will doubtless have your own.

RICHIE BENAUD

My brother John and I were very lucky to have parents who were lovers of cricket. My father, Lou, was one of the finest country cricketers during the Great Depression years in Australia. In 1937 he started playing with Central Cumberland in the club competition, which was the stepping stone to Sheffield Shield cricket.

Our meal times were always taken up with cricket chat and advice and in 1964 he wrote a book, *The Young Cricketer*, still talked about for the good advice it contained. In another manuscript my father headed a chapter 'Cricket – My Cricket' and it began:

> The spirit of cricket: there is something about cricket that one doesn't seem to get so strongly from other games. That something is the spirit of cricket which creates a great love of the game in the heart of the person who is imbued with that spirit.

Three years earlier the Tied Test series was played in Australia and walking off the 'Gabba field after the tied match with Frank Worrell, arms around one another's shoulders, was, for me, the first of two great spirit-of-cricket moments.

> The second was the photograph on the cover of this book; Andrew Flintoff and Brett Lee after England had won the Second Test at Edgbaston in 2005.
>
> Ted Dexter and Colin Cowdrey deserve our thanks and admiration.
>
> *Richie Benaud, Australia 1952–64*
>
> John Benaud played three Tests for Australia in 1972 and 1973, scoring 223 runs at an average of 44.60

Often, of course, the man trying to knock your head off is neither family member nor friend. The spirit of cricket is rarely more alive than when two champions are in pursuit of victory, and then washing it down with a handshake and a cold beer. While cricket is ostensibly a team game, its gift is that it ultimately breaks down into millions of individual contests (or rather 2,700, if we are talking about 450 overs of a five-day Test). Some have an infinitesimal impact upon the game; others *are* the game, whether symbolically or actually.

The duel need not last a long time to reward us – seeing a bowler strike early or a batsman hit someone out of the attack has a thrill of its own – but the best surely comes when the contest has time to develop. It is a window into the soul.

MIKE ATHERTON AND ALLAN DONALD
ENGLAND V SOUTH AFRICA, 4TH TEST, TRENT BRIDGE, 23–27 JULY 1998

Many of cricket's most famous individual duels have existed either in isolation from the wider picture; the beauty of Allan Donald's legendary confrontation with Mike Atherton in 1998 is that it was inextricably linked to the context of the team. It effectively decided both the match and the series. Fittingly, too, for these were two of the most unselfish cricketers of their age, men who sent themselves to the brink of the knacker's yard for the greater good.

For all the physical courage that defined their careers, however, it was the mental strain that was of greater significance here. It was the decisive point of a series that England would win 2–1 despite being almost humiliatingly outplayed for the first half of the series.

Tim de Lisle wrote in *Wisden* that: 'It is a requirement of thriller writing that the hero should be taken almost to the point of no return. At the end of the second act, he (or she) will ideally be clinging to a precipice, in a hurricane, by one finger, while the baddie takes leisurely aim, from a sheltered vantage point, with an automatic weapon. This is precisely the position in which the England cricket team found themselves on July 5–6, 1998.'

That was during the third Test at Old Trafford, which England somehow drew despite following-on. Yet three weeks later – and how weird it feels now to note such a gap between Tests – they were in a position to square the series: chasing 247 in a topsy-turvy match, they moved past 70 for the loss of one wicket on the fourth evening.

Hansie Cronje inevitably called up his go-to bowler, Donald. 'I felt in my bones that the game would be decided by the next few overs,' wrote Donald in his autobiography. Atherton had the same instinct; this may have been the first summer in seven that he was not England captain, but he still wore the burden of the knowledge that, if he failed, so in all probability would England. 'I told myself: this is now the critical period,' he wrote. 'The game will be won or lost here. The responsibility is mine and mine alone.'

After a couple of fierce but relatively uneventful overs, Donald's switch to an around-the-wicket angle was apparently rewarded when Atherton got in a mess against a beautifully directed short ball and palpably gloved it to the wicketkeeper Mark Boucher. The umpire Steve Dunne said not out. 'I couldn't believe my fortune,' wrote Atherton. Donald remained calm. 'I thought, "I'll kill him."'

For the next few overs, it appeared he was trying to do just that. Yet appearances were deceptive: this was a primal duel played out in the head. Both men somehow managed to maintain their composure in the moments that mattered.

Donald offered his four-letter thoughts on Atherton's refusal to walk at every opportunity, but he noticeably composed himself at the start of his run-up, sucking in deep breaths while he cleared his head and decided exactly where the next ball should go. Atherton called on the priceless experience of a bare-knuckle beating at the hands of Courtney Walsh on a Sabina Park slab four-and-a-half years earlier: he willed himself to maintain positive body language and particularly eye contact when Donald was attempting to intimidate him, knowing that it was the bowler who eventually had to go back to his mark.

At the other end, probably a little jealous of Atherton, was Nasser Hussain. 'He was irrelevant to me,' said Donald. Yet he became central to the action when he edged Donald through to Boucher, who dropped a routine chance. Donald let rip a blood-curdling cry of frustration; moments later, he still had the presence to run from fine leg to pat a distraught Boucher, aged 21 and playing only his tenth Test, on the backside.

It had become cricket of the rarest intensity. But Donald could not bowl for ever, and England eventually saw him off. The next day was muted by comparison – how could it not be? – and England breezed to victory by eight wickets, with Atherton there at the end on 98 not out.

This most honourable of contests ended in the time-honoured fashion, with Atherton approaching Donald for a post-match beer. The two discussed the match, with Donald admitting he wouldn't have walked either. Atherton even signed his glove, complete with offending red mark, to be sold during Donald's benefit year. Whoever bought that has quite a souvenir, yet there were millions of beneficiaries of this extraordinarily battle.

South Africa (374 & 208) lost to England (336 & 247-2) by 8 wickets

NASSER HUSSAIN

I was at the other end for the battle between Allan Donald and Mike Atherton at Trent Bridge in 1998. It was great stuff, right on the edge, with a few choice words from Donald in a few different languages. There was a lot of history between the two of them. Not that they hated each other, but that they knew how important the other was to their side. I had the best seat in the house, standing on my bat, making sure I didn't get down Donald's end. Atherton's no mug: he eventually got me on strike. Then Mark Boucher dropped me, and the scream and the eyes and the body language of Donald were unbelievable. Everyone instinctively knew that the game would be decided there and then. I've got a picture at home of me and Ath walking off that evening, and we were thinking: 'We've won this game.'

You could argue that Atherton gloving one to the keeper and not walking is not exactly the highest bit of sportsmanship, but I believe in playing it tough. I wasn't a walker, nor was Atherton, and I make no apologies for that. If I was captain I'd have been fuming if Atherton had walked. Let the umpire make the decision. You get a few good ones and you get a few shockers in your career.

I enjoyed the fact that Atherton was playing it tough, and saying: 'Sorry I've got away with it, but I'm not a walker, I'm playing for my country and the bloke at the other end has given me not out. You can give me all the abuse you want, I understand why you're cross, but I'm going to stick by the Laws of the game.'

The other incredible thing was that it was the flattest pitch of all time. It got flatter as the game went on, and by the end it was an absolute belter. But because he was so angry, Donald got so much more out of that pitch than anyone else. I said to Ath: 'What have you woken this bloke up for?! That's the last thing we need.'

There was a lot of controversy in that series, especially with the umpiring, so there was quite a bit of animosity. You might think Donald would have been effing and blinding after the game, but when it finished the following day he knocked on our dressing-room door, sat between me and Ath and opened a beer. I remember the hour in the dressing-room as vividly as the hour out in the middle. The two of them sat there chatting and laughing about it. That speaks volumes for both men.

Ath is the sort of bloke who enjoys a laugh at other people's misfortune. I remember in Guyana when I hooked Courtney Walsh as hard as I could and was caught by Jimmy Adams, diving forward at short leg; when I got back to the dressing room and I could see Atherton's shoulders going in the corner, giggling at me. So he loved that he got one over on Donald, and the two of them still laugh about it when they see each other. That day, in the dressing room, you wouldn't have known which player had been on the losing side. When those bails go off, you don't hold grudges. I really appreciated that in Allan Donald.

Nasser Hussain, England 1990–2003

The most famous duels, inevitably, involve fast bowler and obstinate batsman. As Donald said of that battle with Atherton: 'I was in such a zone that it was a case of him or me.' The primal element engages on a visceral level, whether it be Brian Close walking fearlessly and absurdly down the wicket to Wes Hall in 1963 – 'when he stripped off in the dressing room his torso looked like a relief map of the Atlas Mountains,' said his teammate Colin Cowdrey – or Dennis Lillee trying to knock Tony Greig's block off in 1974–75 after Greig had goaded him by signalling boundaries and telling Lillee to 'fetch that'.

In that same series came an even more famous contest: Jeff Thomson against Colin Cowdrey. Everything was stacked against Cowdrey, aged 42, yet on this most traumatic of tours for England, he proved he was not just another Pom to the slaughter.

JEFF THOMSON V COLIN COWDREY
AUSTRALIA V ENGLAND, 2ND TEST, PERTH, 13–17 DECEMBER 1974

In the middle of December 1974, in a delightfully snowbound Kent, most were dreaming of a white Christmas. But Colin Cowdrey's love of cricket transcended all else, and his dream was everyone else's worst nightmare: facing Dennis Lillee and Jeff Thomson on Test cricket's bounciest castle, the WACA in Perth.

Cowdrey was 41 and had not played Test cricket for nearly four years when he was summoned to join an England party that was already down to the bare bones after just one Test of Lillee and Thommo, but at no point did he betray anything other than sheer boyish excitement at the opportunity of playing at the highest level again. When he arrived in Australia and was greeted with a number of questions about how a fortysomething would cope with 90mph bowling, he mischievously said: 'I can't believe they are as fast as [Jack] Gregory and [Ted] McDonald in the twenties, and I played them.'

Even though his flight had taken nearly 50 hours, Cowdrey was thrown straight into the second Test in Perth, which started four days after his arrival. Tony Greig recalls Max Walker, the third prong of Australia's fearsome pace attack, saying: 'Lillee and Thommo will kill him stone dead!' Quite the contrary. To everyone else, this tour was becoming an extreme trauma (*Wisden* called it 'the greatest battering in the history of the game') yet to Cowdrey it was great larks.

When he arrived at the crease in the first innings – 'It was the signal for tears to prick the eyes of all but the stony-hearted,' wrote Christopher Martin-Jenkins – he walked up to Thomson, shook his hand and said: 'Good morning, my name's Cowdrey'. It was a like a country gent sauntering into a redneck bar, whipping off his trilby and cheerfully announcing, 'Gentlemen, what a fine day for a haircut.' Yet Cowdrey got unflinchingly behind the ball, taking the inevitable blows without complaint and batting for more than two hours in each innings even though England were again blown away.

He played the remaining Tests and, although he only

managed 165 runs at an average of 18, he achieved something very few of his teammates did on that tour: he earned the Australians' respect.

England (208 & 293) lost to Australia (481 & 23-1) by 9 wickets

An apparently unbalanced contest can be equally riveting. It might be a lower-order batsman getting bravely into line, as Brett Lee did against Andrew Flintoff at Edgbaston in 2005, or even a rank tailender inexplicably surviving, as Monty Panesar did against Australia at Cardiff in 2009. Those moments remind us of cricket's silly charm, as did the sight of David Steele – 'the bank clerk who went to war' – standing up so successfully to Thomson and Lillee in 1975 that he was voted the BBC Sports Personality of the Year.

On other occasions, it really is personal, with the contretemps as much about the two protagonists as the match itself. Malcolm Marshall, for example, persecuted the brilliant Indian batsman Dilip Vengsarkar during India's tour of the Caribbean in 1982–83. Vengsarkar had, Marshall thought, claimed a catch off the pad on his debut four and a half years earlier, and when Marshall was given out for nought he left the field in tears. Most of the time Marshall got his man cheaply but, in the final Test in Antigua, Vengsarkar counter-attacked thrillingly in a manic period before Marshall had him caught on the hook for 94. Even though West Indies had an unassailable 2–0 lead in the series, Marshall said that he had 'never been more elated at a wicket nor so relieved at a dismissal'.

If that was truly cricket in the raw, it is easy to forget that noble duels can be equally rewarding on a subtler, more insidious level. Michael Brearley talks fondly of a contest with the bewitching Indian offspinner Erapalli Prasanna, while the two men and a dog who were in the crowd for the very last first-class game at the United Services Ground in Portsmouth in July 2000 still turn misty-eyed when they recall an unimaginably high-class contest between Hampshire's Shane Warne and Kent's Rahul Dravid. Some regard it as the finest county cricket ever played.

Warne was also part of a glorious duel with Sachin Tendulkar during the 1996 World Cup. He returned figures of 10-1-28-1, and Tendulkar made a thrilling 90 before being stumped, not off Warne but Mark Waugh. Two years later, Tendulkar defenestrated Warne during a mind-blowing unbeaten 155 to win the first Test at Chennai, an ignominy from which Warne arguably never quite recovered when playing on Indian soil.

MICHAEL BREARLEY

Test and county cricket, like many other forms of sport, is a tough business, only really honest when played to win, no quarter given. But there is another side of cricket which can too easily be lost, and that is the playfulness and mutual respect between high-powered, hard competitors. We not only - rightly - want to defeat our opponents, we also depend on them and their skill, courage and hostility in order to excavate and hone our own skills and pride. There is a unity of shared striving, as well as a duality of opposition.

In 1976–77, I was fortunate enough to play five Tests in India. One of India's formidable quartet of spin bowlers was Erapalli Prasanna. He was a short, somewhat rotund offspinner, with large, dark, alert eyes, and a wonderful control of flight. For some reason, I felt that between us this playful element existed. He and I would engage in a kind of eye-play. His look would say: 'OK, you played that one all right, but where will the next one land?' And mine would reply, 'Yes, you fooled me a little, but notice I adjusted well enough.' He had that peculiarly Indian minimal sideways waggle of the head, which suggests that the vertebrae of the sub-continental neck are more loosely linked than in our stiffer Western ones. The waggle joined with the eyes in saying: 'I acknowledge your qualities, and I know that you acknowledge mine.'

I found it easier to enter such an engagement with a slow bowler, who might bamboozle me and get me out, but wasn't going to hurt me. But I had something similar with Robin Jackman, the Surrey and England fast-medium bowler. With him, I could actually enjoy his best ball, which pitched on a perfect length on off stump and moved away. I also enjoyed the fact that it was too good to take the edge of my bat! There was the same friendly rivalry, imbued with mutual respect and humour. The spirit of cricket – or more broadly, of sport – at its best, I think.

Michael Brearley, England 1997

Erapalli Prasanna played 49 Tests for India, collecting 189 wickets at 30.38.

Robin Jackman played 4 Tests for England: he took 14 wickets at 31.78 and more than 1,400 first-class wickets

Warne and Tendulkar's battle would inevitable endure the length of their careers, and the subtle battles for supremacy over a period of time – rather than one isolated spell – can be equally compelling. Ray Lindwall and Len Hutton were engaged in a riveting tug-of-war during their Ashes battles of the forties and fifties, as were Keith Miller and Denis Compton, soulmates off the pitch but the fiercest competitors on it. Their most memorable contest came in the first Test of the Invincibles' tour of 1948. Compton had taken England to the cusp of safety with a marvellous, seven-hour 184, an innings of which *Wisden* said 'No praise could be too high'. It ended when, with ten minutes to go to lunch on the final day, Miller, who bowled 44 overs in the innings, roused himself once more and sent down a vicious bouncer. Compton shaped to hook, realised he could not and, in trying to get out the way, trod on his stumps. Australia won by eight wickets.

Compton and Miller's competitive rivalry lasted a decade from 1946; such extended battles offer the rewarding sight of a player overcome his nemesis, particularly a bowler who has tortured him in the past. In 1989, Graham Gooch was so vulnerable to the wicket-to-wicket interrogation of Terry Alderman that, when somebody scrawled 'THATCHER OUT' on a wall, another wag added 'LBW b Alderman 0'. Yet when the teams reconvened 18 months later, a dismal tour overall for Gooch (he captained a side apparently addicted to collapses, which lost 3–0 despite playing very well for large parts of the series, prompting Gooch to say it was 'like a fart competing with thunder') was partially redeemed by his performance against Alderman, who dismissed him only once.

Most of the time we think of the bowler as the hunter and the batsman as the prey, but the roles have often been reversed, particularly, though not exclusively, since the 21st-century empowerment of batsmen. Such a shift of focus brings its own possibilities. It is hard to imagine a more satisfying dismissal than that of the spin bowler who, having been dumped for six once or twice, continues to toss the ball up and gets his reward. Bishan Bedi made a career of it.

Similarly, it is always entertaining to witness a battle between great players from different generations, an informal passing of the baton. In the 1992 World Cup match between England and India, Ian Botham (aged 36) bowled to Sachin Tendulkar (18) for the only time in international cricket and had him caught behind for 35. At the other end of the scale, an 18-year-old Botham came of age with a matchwinning 45 not out against

Andy Roberts in the Benson & Hedges Cup quarter-final of 1974, despite losing teeth when he was hit by Roberts's quicker bouncer. Then there is the old soak putting an upstart in his place, as with Alec Stewart gleefully pulling Brett Lee to distraction at Sydney in 2002–03, every stroke carrying the implicit message: 'You've got a lot more to achieve in the game, son, before you can bounce me on a flat deck.'

Those roles can be reversed. In a winner-takes-all encounter between Kent and Glamorgan in the 1993 Sunday League, there was a beautiful contest between the lightning-quick Duncan Spencer (aged 21) and Viv Richards (41 and playing his last-ever game at the highest level). Richards and Glamorgan won, but only after he had survived a fearsome working-over from Spencer, who split his batting glove, struck him on the chest and had him caught at short leg off a no-ball. Richards said Spencer was possibly the fastest bowler he had ever faced. Spencer looked destined for greatness. As it turned out he would play only 16 first-class games, but the memory of his contest with Richards endures. As does the spell bowled by Ishant Sharma, just 19 and playing his fourth Test, to the Australian captain Ricky Ponting in India's seismic victory at Perth in 2007–08.

If some great duels have the capacity to kickstart a career, they can also end one. Sonny Ramadhin, the West Indies' mystery offspinner whose variations had befuddled allcomers, was never quite the same after Peter May and Colin Cowdrey nullified him with their pads during their stand of 411 at Edgbaston in 1957. In doing so, they saved the match and demystified a major opponent.

The individual contest was compelling, but the wider context remained the most important thing.

The essence of the noble duel is giving it and being able to take it; playing hard but fair. Rarely has that been in greater evidence than when Douglas Jardine was given a taste of his own Bodyline medicine, in the summer of 1933, by the West Indian pair of Manny Martindale and Learie Constantine in the second Test at Old Trafford. With delicious predictability, Jardine made his only Test century.

MITCHELL JOHNSON

One thing that always sticks in my mind is the handshake between Andrew Flintoff and Brett Lee in 2005. I was in India at the time on a Cricket Academy tour and I thought it was pretty special for Flintoff to console Brett, help him up, shake his hand, look him in the eye and congratulate him for a great performance. That's why Australians have such respect for Flintoff: he's a fierce competitor and a great bowler but also a great guy on and off the field. When it comes to the end of the match he'll look you in the eye and shake your hand, and if you've done well he'll let you know. I was the last batsman out in the Test at Lord's in 2009 and, even though they'd smashed us, he didn't go over the top. He was very sporting.

You should be able to do that: have hard, tough contests with people and then sit down with them at the end of a game or a series.

That way you don't have any problems with each other. Stuart Broad and I had plenty of run-ins during the last Ashes but we sat down and had a good chat at the end of the series. That's what it should be about.

In Australia you get that drilled into your mind through club cricket. When you come through as a young guy there are blokes who are a lot older than you and they play very hard cricket, but at the end of it they sit down and have a beer with the opposition. All the things that have happened on the field mean nothing once you're off it. That's the way Australian cricketers have grown up.

Mitchell Johnson, Australia 2005–

JACQUES KALLIS

To me, the spirit of cricket is reflected in the way I've always tried to play the game: that's to play hard on the field, but at the end of the day or at the end of your career to be able to pick up the phone and call the guy you've played against. That is a good judge of whether you've played in the right way or not. It is tough, tough game, but it's important to keep control of your emotions and not cross the line. As much as anything, it's born of a respect for your opponents and teammates. You want to treat someone the way you want to be treated. That's not to say you can't have a harsh word occasionally, but it's vital that you don't cross the line.

A good example was a contest between Allan Donald and Steve Waugh in Sydney in 1997-98: Allan hit Steve in the ribs a few times, but there was not a lot said, just a few looks and two of the greats fighting it out. That cricket was as hard as I've ever seen, and that's what you look for. I was 22 at the time, and it was an awesome lesson: it made me realise that you don't need words or cheap gestures to get a proper battle going. You don't want a guy shouting his mouth off. The ball and the bat do the work. Words have never got a wicket. I would like to believe that I've been true to that - I've never had trouble with match referees or anything like that - and that I would able to pick up the phone and call most of the players that I've played against.

Jacques Kallis, South Africa 1995–

Constantine and Martindale might have seemed a couple of dobbers compared to what Steve Waugh faced in Trinidad in 1994-95. On a horrible, seaming pitch that would produce only 467 runs for 31 wickets, Waugh responded to the menacing stare of Curtly Ambrose by asking him, in marginally less polite terms, what the devil he was looking at. 'He stood his ground like John Wayne,' said *Wisden*. Ambrose had to be restrained by his captain, Richie Richardson; Waugh, showing a mental strength that most of us could barely imagine, never mind replicate, made an unbeaten 63 out of a first-innings total of 128.

Not that either aspect – Steve Waugh riling a West Indian paceman, or an Australian batsman riling Curtly Ambrose – has always been successful. When Waugh, in those days a slippery medium-pacer, repeatedly bounced Patrick Patterson towards the end of the fourth day of the 1988 Boxing Day Test in Melbourne, Patterson walked into the Australian dressing room at the close of play and calmly informed everyone that he would kill them out in the middle tomorrow. In the end he settled for 5-39 and a crushing victory.

Similarly, when Dean Jones engaged Ambrose's wick by complaining about his wristbands during a one-day match at Melbourne in 1988–89, it backfired hideously. The umpires forced Ambrose to remove his wristbands; rags don't come any redder, and he bludgeoned Australia to defeat with 5-17.

Such absurd misjudgements are part of cricket's charm. It is a sport that has always felt comfortable laughing itself. At the same time, it is certainly hard to envisage another game in which a leading figure would describe the impassioned celebration of reaching a century as 'Just bad manners, if the truth be told' (Ted Dexter, 1998). In days of yore, milestones were met with little more than a manly handshake and, if you were feeling particularly frisky, a smidgin of eye contact. When Jim Laker became the first man to take all ten wickets in a Test innings, against Australia in 1956, he simply spun on his heels and took his sweater from the umpire, a fact we can only partly attribute to Laker's innate modesty. 'The quiet style,' wrote Colin Cowdrey, 'has always seemed to me to be the right way to carry one's talents.' Sometimes that was a product of simple shyness. 'I much preferred the ordeal of facing Australian bowling,' said Jack Hobbs in his autobiography, 'to that of facing a jubilant English crowd.'

Things change, inevitably, and while some modern celebrations may verge on the vulgar – Usman Afzaal's delirious air-punching when he reached his first Test fifty, against Australia in 2001, seemed absurd at the time and utterly ridiculous when he was out a few minutes later – others have a cuteness that belongs to the spirit of cricket: in that same summer of 2001, for example, Glenn McGrath introduced the culture of bowlers politely holding the ball up to the crowd upon taking a five-for.

Restraint in the moment of triumph remains a fascinating and admirable quality, as shown by the joyous public reaction to Andrew Flintoff's embrace with Brett Lee at Edgbaston in 2005, but the response to adversity is arguably even more telling. When Essex's Graham Napier scored an astonishing 152 not out from 58 balls, with 16 sixes, in 2008, the Sussex wicketkeeper Matt Prior ignored the fact that his team were being pummelled and gave Napier a big bear-hug. It was voted the MCC spirit of cricket moment for 2008.

ANDREW FLINTOFF AND BRETT LEE
ENGLAND V AUSTRALIA, 2ND TEST, EDGBASTON,
4–7 AUGUST 2005

In many walks of life, man is judged by the physical strength of his handshake. The cricket world certainly judged Andrew Flintoff and Brett Lee by the moral strength of theirs at Edgbaston in 2005, and came to the unanimous verdict that they were two of the most admirable sportsmen around.

Forget the 182 wickets that were blown like confetti across the unforgettable summer of 2005: that Ashes series was defined by their embrace at the end of the second Test at Edgbaston. There have been maybe a dozen truly great series in Test cricket history, but arguably the two that most stand out – Australia v West Indies in 1960–61 and England v Australia in 2005 – do so because they combined peaks of excellence with an overwhelming chivalry. Flintoff and Lee became the poster boys for a series that oozed goodwill.

Their show of sportsmanship was all the more splendid for what had gone before. On an unforgettable Sunday morning at Edgbaston, with the Ashes in the balance, Flintoff and Lee had engaged in a one-way bare-knuckle brawl, with Flintoff landing blow after blow on his man. Australia were 1–0 up; if England were to go 2–0 down, they could theoretically have won 3–2, but the psychological implications of defeat would have made that almost impossible.

Australia needed 104 runs with two wickets remaining; in England, victory was thus perceived as a formality. Yet that morning, as the church bells rang for Sunday service around the country, the death knell began to toll for England. First Lee and Shane Warne, and then Lee and the number 11 Michael Kasprowicz, inched Australia towards an unlikely win.

Lee faced 75 deliveries from Flintoff, approximately 75 of which struck him on the body. Flintoff simply pummelled Lee, marking his torso with so many bruises that it was left looking like a grotesque piece of modern art. Ironically matters were decided at the other end, when Steve Harmison dismissed Kasprowicz to win the game for England by two runs. So ended one of the epics of Test cricket – only one game in 132 years has been won by fewer runs – yet as the England team celebrated the surreal feeling of winning a live Ashes Test, Flintoff went straight to his opponent in a moment of the richest humanity.

Look at the picture: the key thing was that moment between Flintoff offering his hand and Lee accepting it. There was every chance that either might crack, that Lee might have misinterpreted the gesture and aggressively brushed away his hand, or that Flintoff might have betrayed his joy with the merest hint of a smile. Neither did, because they knew the importance of the moment. They were also, you suspect, aware that what had gone before was not as significant as what was to come; that an already intoxicating series had moved to another level entirely, on both a sporting and human level. Flintoff's face is a mixture of compassion, comradeship and even confusion that sport could engender such emotions. Lee's face conveys empathy, gratitude, surprise and the weariness of a man who had just been a punch bag for Flintoff. As with their earlier battle, all of this was instinctive and unspoken.

And then they *did* speak. We will probably never know exactly what they said to each other during that embrace, but it's best that way. It adds a romantic, cinematic charm. We will be left to wonder what they said.

What they achieved was easier to discern. They had served to dignify the undignifiable in a manner in which it is not too trite to say there were no losers.

England, of course, went on to win the series, with Flintoff lording over proceedings like a cartoon superhero. Lee, along with the remarkable Shane Warne, became the Aussie it was okay to like. His cherubic smile, enormous pride and grace in the face of imminent defeat helped define the final few Tests. Lee actually averaged over 40 with the ball in that series – not a flattering statistical performance, but one that scarcely matters. He is one of the faces of the series, and one half of cricket's signature handshake.

England (407 & 182) beat Australia (308 & 279) by 2 runs

ANDREW FLINTOFF

Andrew Flintoff is charisma incarnate. Even if he were not one of the greatest all-round cricketers England has produced, he would be a spectacular human being: magnetic, gregarious, quick-witted and blessed with the unusual combination of self-deprecation and strong self-assurance.

His England Test career split neatly into three acts. From the 1998 to 2003, he struggled to understand his body and how to get the returns for all his hard work – particularly with the ball – in international cricket. From 2003 to 2006 he seemed able to turn water into wine on demand, most notably during the 2005 Ashes series, when he cast as big a shadow over the series as Ian Botham had in 1981. And since the summer of 2006 he has struggled to cope with the regular breakdown of a body that has been flogged mercilessly for the cause.

In that respect, Flintoff's sporting career has suffered because of his good nature. Giving his all has taken its toll. But then, as his millions of disciples would tell you, Flintoff's personality was always an integral part of the package.

When Matt Prior gave Graham Napier that bear hug, his love of the game transcended all else. So did that of the great Bishen Bedi, who frequently clapped batsman who hit him down the ground for six.

Ricky Ponting won the respect and admiration of most of England with his outstanding conduct during the 2009 Ashes. Despite being booed when he walked out to bat, and despite a series defeat that must have felt somewhere between unfortunate and grand larceny, Ponting was always gracious and even made a point of going down to the Long Room at Lord's to shake every England player's hand after Australia had lost the second Test.

When his Test record of 365 was overtaken by Brian Lara in Antigua in 1994, Garry Sobers appeared proudly on the field to embrace his successor. Lara then sent a note of congratulations to Matthew Hayden, who extended the record to 380, before taking it back himself a few months later.

STEVE WAUGH
AUSTRALIA V INDIA, 2ND TEST, ADELAIDE, 12–16 DECEMBER 2003

With that merciless, cold stare of his, Steve Waugh seemed like the last person who cared about the opposition. Yet for all his furious desire to win, Waugh always had half an eye on the bigger picture: whether it was his rare fascination with the history of the game, his desire to look beyond cricket – most notably when he took the Australian team on a pilgrimage to Gallipoli in 2001 – or just his appreciation of excellence, whether it be from teammate or opponent.

The best example of the latter came after the Adelaide Test against India in 2003. Despite scoring 556 in the first innings Australia were beaten by four wickets, thanks mainly to one of the great performances from Rahul Dravid, who made 233 and 72 not out and batted for nearly 14 hours in the match. When he cut Stuart MacGill for four to seal India's first Test win in Australia for 23 years, Waugh chased it to the boundary, picked it out of the gutter and handed it to Dravid before saying simply, 'Well played, mate.'

This was partly born of a mutual respect that began almost six years earlier when, during Australia's tour of India, a young Dravid went for a meal with Waugh and picked his brain incessantly on the mental aspect of the game. Dravid's performance at Adelaide certainly had a granite will that Waugh would have recognised, and a sheer class he probably secretly envied. In his autobiography, Waugh described Dravid's performance as 'poetic, with flowing follow-throughs . . . His head was like the statue of David, allowing for perfect balance and easy hand-eye coordination.'

Waugh's reaction was not simply because Dravid was a friend. If he saw something he liked, even in a well-beaten foe, he would say so. In 2001, while most of England was opining that Paul Collingwood was completely out of his depth after he had scored a mere 20 runs in four innings in his debut one-day series, Waugh said that Collingwood had something about him. It was a comment that, Collingwood later said, infused him with a vital self-belief on his slow journey to the top.

In the case of Dravid, the historian in Waugh also recognised that beautiful moment when a player moves from very good to great, and knew it should be marked accordingly. And while he may have been almost pathologically incapable of losing, Waugh knew *how* to lose: with dignity and class. His gesture was even more admirable in this instance because of the personal context. It was Waugh's farewell series, and India's victory meant there was a very real chance that Waugh's career would end with Australia losing their first series at home for 15 years. Most players would have been preoccupied with that, certainly in the aftermath of such a numbing defeat. But then Waugh always looked beyond the immediate context.

Australia (556 & 196) lost to India (523 & 233-6) by four wickets

CHAPTER TWO

As with so many of the things that inform our understanding of the spirit of cricket, there are apparent contradictions. Kim Hughes was widely ridiculed for weeping when he resigned as Australian captain in 1984; as time has moved on, and notions of masculinity have evolved, it is now seen by many as a natural human reaction. Few sneered when Michael Vaughan cried upon resigning as England captain in 2008.

Muttiah Muralitharan never shed tears, publicly at least, in the darker times when he was demonised for supposedly being a chucker, most notably when he was humiliatingly no-balled seven times in three overs by Darrell Hair during the MCG Test of 1995–96. Murali's sheer decency – his refusal to respond to often vicious abuse, his unbreakable smile, his omnipresent enthusiasm – is the very essence of the spirit of cricket.

At the end of 2009, Cricinfo's Rob Steen nominated Murali as the greatest 'Joybringer' of the decade. 'An underdog and outsider with a social conscience and magic at his fingertips: no sportsman has ever brought me greater joy,' wrote Steen. When Muralitharan was named the Leading Cricketer in the World in the *Wisden Cricketers' Almanack* of 2007, Simon Barnes wrote that: 'The time has come to grasp the nettle . . . to reject the frown, the shrug, the pursed lips and the quizzical look . . . Muralitharan is a truly great cricketer, and those that cannot go along with such a sentiment have something lacking in their souls. The spirit of cricket, perhaps.'

For much of his career, Murali has been a one-man bowling attack. Between 2000 and 2006 he took an outrageous 39 per cent of the Test wickets taken by Sri Lankan bowlers. That would be an outrageous achievement in one series; over a seven-year period, it beggars belief.

Watching a player carry a team, or excel in an obviously lost cause, is to witness a glorious demonstration of the human spirit. Such a phenomenon is particularly acute in the case of Brian Lara. Like Murali, Lara often seemed to be a one-man team; yet whereas Sri Lanka have been on an upward curve during Murali's career, West Indies plummeted dismally during Lara's time. When he made his Test debut in Pakistan in 1990–91, West Indies were undeniably the best team in the world; when he played his final Test, in Pakistan 16 years later, they were eighth in the world rankings, above only Bangladesh and Zimbabwe.

Through it all Lara continued to play with devastating freedom and reel off huge, potentially match-winning centuries. The problem was that, because the bowlers almost always were unable to back him up, the speed at which he scored was frequently not match-winning but match-losing. At the end of his Test career no other player in the game's history had made more than 3,059 in defeats. Lara made 5,316. In the 2000s alone, he played eight innings in excess of 150 in defeat. Often his team were not just beaten, but thrashed. To continue to play such worthless epics showed remarkable strength, and when Lara retired his role was taken by Shivnarine Chanderpaul, who averaged over 100 in Tests in both 2007 and 2008.

Virender Sehwag, who bats in a bubble entirely of his own, is also adept at making runs regardless of the success or otherwise of his teammates, but even he will struggle to match the performance of his countryman Vijay Hazare, who made 309 out of a total of 387 for Hindus in 1943–44.

VIJAY HAZARE
HINDUS V THE REST, BOMBAY PENTANGULAR TOURNAMENT
FINAL, BOMBAY, 3–6 DECEMBER 1943

At first it seems like a riddle, or a trick question: '*Team A score 581 in their only innings. Team B lose by an innings, even though one of their batsmen scores 309 in the second innings. Detail a credible scenario whereby this is possible.*' Perhaps there was contrivance; a dodgy declaration. Or perhaps there was one remarkable performance from Vijay Hazare.

When The Rest were hammered by Hindus in the final of the prestigious Bombay Pentangular Tournament in 1943, Hazare, who was once described by Fred Trueman as being 'as good a player of fast bowling as there was in the world', scored 309 out of a total of 387. That accounted for 79.84 per cent of his team's score, but Hazare actually scored 309 out of 354 runs off the bat while he was at the crease – an absurd 87 per cent. He had a partnership of 300 for the sixth wicket with his brother Vivek. Vijay contributed 266, Vivek 21.

Hazare also top-scored in the first innings with 59 out of 133 and bowled 51 overs of medium-pace cutters, taking three of the five Hindus wickets to fall. Even though Hazare was emphatically on the losing side, there was a beautiful subplot to his personal achievement. Earlier in the month he had scored 248, taking Vijay Merchant's record for the highest-ever score in the Bombay Pentangular. Merchant responded with 250 in the first innings of this match, and then Hazare went one – or rather 59 – better later in the game.

His innings came as part of one of the purplest patches imaginable: in first-class cricket in 1943, Hazare's scores were 264, 81, 97, 248, 59, 309, 101 and 223. Über-Bradman stuff.

'We lost the match but then the crowd rushed to the pavilion at the Brabourne Stadium, broke some of the chairs, and they wanted me to come out,' remembered Hazare. 'Merchant took me out and asked me to tell them that we would be meeting again in the Ranji Trophy next week. So I told the crowd, I'll be playing the next match against Bombay at the Brabourne Stadium on such and such a day. Please do come and watch.'

After such a performance, they could scarcely fail to.

Hindus (581-5 dec) beat The Rest (133 & 387) by an innings and 61 runs

Individuals can be compelling viewing even if their contribution is minimal. Cricket has always had its share of mavericks. There are enough to fill a book on their own; when *Wisden* settled for a list of the top 50 in 2008, pride of place went to (in reverse order) Brian Close, Keith Miller, Roy Gilchrist, Douglas Jardine and, of course, W. G. Grace. Everyone will have their favourite, from the current era and the self-confessed six-addict, Shahid Afridi, all the way back to the end of the 19th century and the South African wicketkeeper Ernest Austin 'Barberton' Halliwell. In modern times, Pakistan have often fielded 11 in the same side. It's hard to think of any other sporting team which so consistently eschews the entire middle ground between the sublime and the ridiculous.

Others include Sultan Zarawani, the United Arab Emirates captain who came out to face Allan Donald at the 1996 World Cup without a helmet and was inevitably sconed first ball; Andrew Hilditch hooking with gay abandon during the 1985 Ashes, even though the stroke cost him his wicket almost every innings; and the (possibly apocryphal) story of John Crawley taking up smoking purely to lose weight after he was savaged by Australian crowds for his slovenly fielding on the 1994–95 tour.

Cricket has never needed much excuse to laugh at itself. The prolonged nature of matches allows for humour to emerge as the contest peters out. In a routine one-day victory over Zimbabwe at Harare in 1995–96, the South African fast bowler Fanie de Villiers bowled the first ball of the final over with a paper cup. In the late seventies and early eighties, Graham Gooch enlivened the final overs of dead Tests with some eerily good pastiches of the bowling action of the likes of Bob Willis. And when Ian Botham bowled the final ball of his career to Australia's David Boon in 1993, Boon was unable to follow the basic batting rule of watching the ball, because he was transfixed by the sight of Botham's genitalia.

The exposure of body parts on the cricket field was not always such a laughing matter for Botham. In 1974, at the age of 18, he lost one tooth and had another split clean in half by a bouncer from the great West Indies' quick bowler Andy Roberts in a memorable B&H Cup quarter-final against Hampshire. Botham ignored the mild concussion, spat the tooth out and led Somerset to a stunning one-wicket victory; it was the surest sign that he was made of the right stuff. As Botham said himself, 'The first chapter of the fairytale was written.'

Displays of physical courage in cricket's history are legendary and legion. Where do we begin? Perhaps with Steve Waugh confounding all reasonable estimates of recovery time for calf injuries and willing himself to a century on one leg against England – in a dead rubber, too – at The Oval in 2001. Or with Eddie Paynter, leaping out of his hospital bed to help England win the Ashes in 1932–33. Colin Cowdrey, the quintessence of the spirit of cricket, gave perhaps the most famous display of physical courage when he came out to bat with a broken arm against West Indies at Lord's in 1963. And Rick McCosker and Anil Kumble both played significant roles in Tests despite suffering broken jaws.

EDDIE PAYNTER
AUSTRALIA V ENGLAND, 4TH TEST, BRISBANE, 10–16 FEBRUARY 1933

Pyjama cricket did not begin with Kerry Packer and World Series Cricket. Eddie Paynter, the brilliant Lancashire left-hander whose average of 84.42 in Ashes Tests is England's highest, played a decisive role in England's Bodyline series victory straight after emerging from his hospital bed and entering the ground in his pyjamas.

England led 2–1 with two to play going into the fourth Test at Brisbane, and Paynter, who had batted with a bad ankle at number 10 against medical advice in the previous Test, was taken to hospital with acute tonsillitis after the first day's play. All reports suggested he had approximately 0.00 per cent chance of batting in the first innings. Paynter, and his unyielding captain Douglas Jardine, had other ideas.

When England slipped to 198-5, a deficit of 142, Paynter left his hospital bed and got a taxi to the Gabba. He was out in the middle at the fall of the next wicket, with the score 216-6, and even refused the offer of a runner. Despite the debilitating heat, Paynter held on till the close, when he was 24 not out, and returned to his hospital bed.

'I'll never forget his face,' said Harold Larwood, who batted with Paynter that evening. 'He looked white and ill. At no time a great talker, he had even less to say that day than usual. He had the shakes. He remained pale throughout but never wavered. I also

67

recall how considerate [Australian captain] Bill Woodfull was to him every moment of his innings.'

The next day Paynter, the personification of the strong, silent type, went on to reach a remarkable 83 in nearly four hours. It gave England an unexpected first-innings lead and, ultimately, an Ashes-winning six-wicket victory. Not that Paynter's work was done. He even fielded in the second innings, and on the sixth day of the match he hit the six that clinched both the Test and the series.

Australia (340 & 175) lost to England 356 & 162-4) by six wickets

There is an understandable tendency to focus on specific matches, but physical courage can equally be displayed over a period of time, whether it's a chronic injury or a ravaged spinning finger. 'Jim Laker's spinning finger was such a bloody mess,' said Ted Dexter, 'all calloused with bloody great holes in it, which were padded out with gunge and goo to get him through the day.' The spinning finger was not Fred Titmus's greatest wound: he overcame the loss of four toes in a hideous boating accident to continue at the highest level. The Nawab of Pataudi made most of his Test runs after losing an eye.

Uncomplaining toil has been evident in so many bowlers: prominent examples include Keith Miller – whose indefatigable performance at Lord's in 1956, when he took 10-152 from 70.1 overs, led to Richie Benaud dubbing it 'Miller's Match' – Andrew Flintoff, and Merv Hughes, who for a while became a one-man seam attack when Craig McDermott was taken ill with appendicitis during the 1993 Ashes tour. Hughes effectively bowled himself into retirement for the Baggy Green. At least he was coming to the end of his international career; David 'Syd' Lawrence's was just beginning when he suffered an horrific, career-wrecking injury at Wellington in 1991–92. In the last hour of a dead rubber that was drifting towards a draw, Lawrence, the Gloucestershire and England fast bowler, continued to bustle in at full pelt, fuelled by a cocktail of pride and patriotism. The consequence was shocking: he fractured his kneecap in delivery stride, precipitating the sort of blood-curdling howl that never fully leaves those who hear it. At the age of 28, his career was effectively over.

Other players seemed to almost revel in the pain. Brian Close, famously, had a threshold so high as to confound all medical assumptions. He would field fearlessly at short leg, dismissing concerns for his welfare with a gruff 'How can the ball hurt you? It's only on you a few seconds.' When, at the age of 45, he was given a chilling working-over from Michael Holding and Andy Roberts on a dark, dangerous Saturday evening at Old Trafford in 1976, he actually looked like he was enjoying it as he let the ball strike his body as often as his bat.

Close was palpably (and probably mercifully) one of a kind, but others have shared his contempt for physical weakness. Robin Smith combined that with an adrenalin-junkie's desire for risk-taking. 'It wasn't a macho thing,' Smith said. 'I just loved the excitement and the adrenalin of not wearing a visor and knowing if you made a mistake you could get seriously hurt. Pain just doesn't bother me. What's the definition of pain? Pain is blokes I know getting bayonets stuck into their thighs and calves during the Rhodesian War. A little cricket ball hardly compares.' When, halfway through his England career, he was asked to pick the highlight, he chose none of the seven Test centuries he had made at that stage but a pre-tea mini-session in Antigua in 1990. Facing Ian Bishop and Courtney Walsh, Smith made 0 from 14 balls – almost all of them bouncers – and had his jaw broken. 'It's the only one of my innings I've ever wanted to keep on video,' he said. 'It was unbelievably exhilarating.'

Smith was clearly roused by pain; Gordon Greenidge was positively liberated by it. He was dangerous on two legs and deadly on one, when an inability to run freely would lead him to deal almost exclusively in boundaries. A coruscating 214 not out at Lord's in 1984, when England were thrashed by nine wickets after declaring their second innings in the expectation of victory, was the principal example.

It was impossible to ignore Greenidge, as he hopped around and sent England hopping mad. Mental courage inevitably takes a more subtle form, but can be an equally vivid demonstration of the spirit of cricket. The charm of players excelling in a lost cause has already been discussed, but perhaps the most obvious sub-genre is that of the career-saving innings. When the Australian skipper Mark Taylor scored 129 in the second innings of the first Test at Edbgaston in 1997, to end a run of 21 Test innings without even a half-century, only the most blindly patriotic Englishman did not admire his courage and dignity.

A different facet of mental courage is in evidence when

watching a batsman plough on despite being in obviously poor form. The England opener John Edrich's 310 not out against New Zealand on a typically grassy Headingley track in 1965 was a perverse cocktail of false strokes and thumping boundaries, with 238 of his runs coming via 52 fours and five sixes. 'I am convinced I shall never see another innings like it,' wrote Colin Cowdrey, who sat padded up while Edrich and Ken Barrington added 369 for the second wicket, more than New Zealand managed in both innings combined. 'It revealed the temperament of a man capable of divorcing from his mind a wild passing shot played only seconds ago, and concentrating on the next ball as a completely new challenge.' Graham Gooch's 114 against New Zealand on a dodgy Auckland pitch in 1991–92 was a bizarre, frequently turgid and undeniably match-winning innings. His capacity to view the past as prologue and concentrate on the next delivery proved vital. It was a glorious display of mental strength.

Six months earlier, Gooch had shown that mental strength again, this time during the finest innings in his career and indeed one of the most remarkable in Test history. Gooch's triumphant 154 not out against a West Indies attack of Malcolm Marshall, Curtly Ambrose, Courtney Walsh and Patrick Patterson – made out of a total of just 252 and with only two other batsmen reaching double figures – was a masterpiece of bristling defiance in the face of a lively pitch and a remorseless attack. That defiance reached its peak when, on the third evening, Gooch declined an offer of the light. Quite how his partner, Derek Pringle, felt about this is anyone's guess (although Pringle went on to survive 144 minutes for 27 in a vital seventh-wicket partnership of 98); either way, it was a gloriously symbolic moment that showed England were no longer afraid of the West Indies. Two days later, they beat them in a Test at home for the first time in 22 years.

When, in 2008, South Africa won a series in England for the first time in 43 years, they did so thanks to another epic 154 not out, this time from their captain Graeme Smith in the third Test at Edgbaston. During that final innings, Andrew Flintoff was wreaking havoc from the Pavilion End, with the batsmen unable to pick up his yorker because of the dark seats above the sightscreen. Neil McKenzie and Jacques Kallis had fallen in vaguely farcical circumstances when Smith decided that enough was enough. Leading the only way he knows, by example, he simply refused to allow anyone else to face Flintoff for the rest of his spell.

When the 42-year-old Colin Cowdrey first walked to the middle in Perth in 1974–75, his partner David Lloyd – whom he scarcely knew – volunteered to take the strike against Dennis Lillee and leave Cowdrey to face the marginally less taxing Max Walker while he found his feet. 'David did exactly that for three consecutive overs,' wrote Cowdrey in his autobiography. 'What a generous thing to do!"

Mental courage in cricket can take so many alternative forms: it might be Courtney Walsh toiling uncomplainingly into the wind for the first nine years and 58 Tests of his career before he finally graduated to senior, new-ball status; or a batsman formulating a plan and sticking rigidly to it, like Gooch playing the sweep almost exclusively during his matchwinning century against India in the 1987 World Cup semi-final.

The capacity of a player to adapt his game, whether for the short or long term, has always been in evidence. In 1984–85, Ravi Shastri clouted the fastest double-century in history, in just 113 minutes, for Baroda against Bombay; a week earlier he had made a seven-hour hundred against England at Calcutta.

For those less flexible than Shastri, it takes enormous bravery and dedication to change a template that has already been so successful. Two of the game's true batting greats, Jack Hobbs and Sachin Tendulkar, pared their game down in their thirties and became even more productive; South Africa's Neil McKenzie, a flighty dasher in the early part of his career, also turned gamekeeper in his thirties. The New Zealand opener Glenn Turner went the other way, reinventing himself as an attacking opener in the 1970s. His teammate Sir Richard Hadlee studied his craft forensically until he made himself an outstanding bowler: in the first six years of his Test career, his bowling average was a modest 31.58; for the final 11 years it was a startling 19.88.

Then there are those who, because of age, were forced to substitute brawn for brain: Dennis Lillee and Malcolm Marshall, in particular, were such formidably intelligent bowlers that a loss of pace had little impact on their performance. To adapt a football cliche, the first five miles per hour were in their head.

Finally there are those who undergo a complete about-face. Mark Richardson started as a number 11 who bowled left-arm spin. When he suffered an attack of the yips, he focused on his batting to such an extent that he stealthily crept up the order and eventually became a highly effective and almost majestically obdurate opening batsman.

Dull cricket might not really be in the spirit, even if is legitimate to argue that there is something admirable about a player who goes so defiantly against the grain, as Richardson did in an age when opening batsmen were just starting to enjoy themselves. The trail was blazed by Saeed Anwar and Michael Slater, although Sanath Jayasuriya and then Virender Sehwag went even further. All four were shamelessly attacking cricketers, scarcely capable of *thinking* about an alternative approach, never mind practising it.

Everyone will have their favourite attacking cricketer, and doing justice to them all is simply impossible here. There are so many stories that demonstrate attacking cricket as an ingrained belief: David Gower lazily pulling his first ball in Test cricket for four; Sri Lanka's openers, Jayasuriya and Romesh Kaluwitharana, both being caught at third man *in the first over* of the 1996 World Cup semi-final; Shahid Afridi, who scored a 37-ball hundred in his first international innings at the age of 16; Sehwag going to India's first Test triple-century with a six; the late David Hookes's manic, angry century from only 34 balls for South Australia against Victoria in 1982, a response to a niggardly declaration from his opposite number Graham Yallop. South Australia were set 272 in 30 overs; Hookes promoted himself to opener and took out his frustration on the Victoria attack. Until he was dismissed, his side were well on course for one of the great victories.

74

Frustrated responses to the negativity of others are not always successful. Garry Sobers' infamous declaration at Trinidad at 1968 cost the West Indies a Test and a series against England but, given his intractable commitment to positive cricket, he probably wouldn't have changed a thing.

SIR GARFIELD SOBERS
WEST INDIES V ENGLAND, 4TH TEST, TRINIDAD
14–19 MARCH 1968

It is the biggest of the few black marks on Sir Garfield Sobers's career, yet there is so much more to his infamous declaration against England in 1967–68 than a match-losing misjudgement. By the accepted means of assessing a declaration at the time – that it should entirely shut out the prospect of defeat – Sobers got it wrong, particularly as he was down to three main bowlers because of an injury to Charlie Griffith. But he was motivated by something more important than avoiding defeat: trying to win.

Sobers was affronted by the tedium of a series that was deadlocked at 0–0, and could not abide the negativity of England's first-innings batting, when they made 404 in 175.4 overs that were most notable for the grass that grew on the outfield. He thus set England 215 to win in just under three hours; or, as it turned out, 54 overs. (The splendid over-rate shows that there was no attempt to slow things down to secure a draw, as Desmond Haynes did against England on the same ground 22 years later.)

It was such an inviting target that even Geoff Boycott went for it, anchoring England's victory with an unbeaten 80. They won with eight balls to spare, and Sobers was the first of only two captains (the other is Graeme Smith) to lose a Test after declaring twice. Given his motivation for the decision, it should really be a badge of honour.

West Indies (526-7 dec & 92-2 dec) lost to England (404 & 215-3) by 7 wickets

Part of Sobers's commitment to attack found expression through his wrist spin, an art forever associated with aggressive cricket. In recent times we have had Stuart MacGill, a man who you suspect would have preferred to take 2-120 than 1-20, but the ultimate embodiment of the attacking legspinner – and perhaps the attacking cricketer per se – was the great Arthur Mailey, a man who, in the words of Richie Benaud, 'wanted to spin the leather off the ball'. It is apt that Mailey is the only Australian to have taken nine wickets in a Test innings; apt too that he conceded 121 runs in so doing, for this was a man who hunted wickets to the exclusion of everything else.

Offensive cricket and aesthetic cricket usually go hand in hand, or wrist on wrist. While there is much to admire is, say, the unimpeachability of Geoffrey Boycott's forward defensive, it is invariably the attackers who know how to shiver the spine and engage the hairs of the back of the neck. No brow could have remained furrowed after the sight of David Gower's creamy cover-drive, while all were powerless to resist the languid rubber-wristed genius of Kumar Ranjitsinhji or Mark Waugh. Then there is V. V. S. Laxman; dubbed 'Very Very Special' by the Australians, who have an entirely justified obsession with him, at his best he takes cricket so far into the realms of art that it is hard to know where one stops and the other begins.

Bowlers and fielders can be equally compelling viewing. The feline grace of Michael Holding's run up brought the nickname 'Whispering Death', while Bishan Bedi's seductive, hissing left-arm spin had an otherworldly quality. Then there are wicketkeepers. Alan Knott's technique was a thing of beauty, while it was said that the Australian Bert Oldfield 'could flick a bail from its groove as a dandy might whisk a speck of snuff from his jacket'.

In the field we might be drawn to Colin Bland, peerless in the covers for South Africa in the sixties, or Jonty Rhodes, the man who flew through the air to run out Inzamam-ul-Haq at the 1992 World Cup and spent the next decade catching flies and turning a quick single into a fatal one. Then there is the West Indian offspinner Roger Harper, who at 6ft 5ins possessed a glorious, muscular athleticism whether in the deep, at backward point or even off his own bowling: his run-out of Graham Gooch in the 1987 Bicentenary Test is as terrifying as anything you will find in cricket.

Advancements in fielding, even since Harper's day, have been simply staggering. And, for a fusty old game, cricket offers a pretty neat line in innovation. The list is almost endless: the googly, the doosra, reverse swing, helmets, the slower ball, the reverse sweep; all the way through to the Dilscoop at the 2009 World Twenty20. Yet such developments have often been seen to be against the spirit of cricket. New, unorthodox shots are sometimes criticised as being an affront to the MCC coaching manual. And when Bernard Bosanquet introduced the googly it was seen as an unfair deception.

Nearly a century later, Dermot Reeve tried to repel Hampshire's left-arm spinner Raj Maru by sporadically dropping his bat so that he could not be given out caught off the glove. And the earpiece worn by the South African Hansie Cronje in their first match of the 1999 World Cup – connected to the coach Bob Woolmer, not his bookie – was promptly outlawed by the ICC. Few would argue with that decision, yet other inventions that have had widespread approval have also brought criticism. Nearly two decades after his retirement, Viv Richards still insists that helmets should not be used and that batsmen should drop their 'suit of armour'.

BERNARD BOSANQUET PLAYS TWISTI-TWOSTI
1897

While there is an understandable romantic inclination to envisage innovations being developed in darkened laboratories by inscrutable geniuses functioning on 30 minutes' sleep per day, the reality is frequently much more mundane. Take the googly, cricket's first Machiavellian skill: its creator Bernard Bosanquet stumbled across it while playing the parlour game Twisti-Twosti, which involved bouncing a ball on a table so that it would elude the person at the other end. 'After a little experimenting I managed to pitch the ball which broke in a certain direction; then with more or less the same delivery make the next ball go in the opposite direction!' wrote Bosanquet. 'I practised the same thing with a soft ball at "Stump-cricket". From this I progressed to the cricket ball . . .'

After three years of practice in the nets, Bosanquet unveiled his googly in 1900. The first batsman to be dismissed by it was Samuel Coe, who had made 98 for Leicestershire against Middlesex when he was stumped by a googly that bounced four times. It was soon also known as the Bosie or the wrong'un, and would became the legspinner's best friend (even though the greatest of them all, Shane Warne, had no sort of wrong'un at all). In the early years, right-handers would play a textbook cover-drive, only to lose their off stump, with bewildering frequency.

It seems absurd now, but the deception intrinsic to the googly's success made it unpopular when it was unveiled: many a previously spoilt batsman regarded it as against the spirit of cricket. 'It is not unfair,' retorted Bosanquet, 'only immoral.' Any attempt to hoodwink an opponent – flipper, doosra, slower ball, effort ball, reverse swing – owes its existence to the Bosie.

WASIM AKRAM TO ROBERT CROFT
ENGLAND V PAKISTAN, 3RD TEST, THE OVAL,
22–26 AUGUST 1996

Action replays are supposed to reduce confusion, not exacerbate it. But when Wasim Akram bowled one of his many contenders for ball of the century at Robert Croft in 1996, the first couple of replays made most viewers even less sure of what had happened. Eventually it became clear: Wasim, from around the wicket, speared a low full toss towards the pads of the right-handed Croft, but it was swung so viciously – and so late – that it comfortably beat the *outside* edge of Croft's bat before pinning him in front of middle stump. Wasim was apoplectic, because he knew it was plumb LBW. But then he knew what he was capable of; for the rest, this was mind-boggling.

Just as commentators often say that great deliveries are wasted on bad batsmen, who aren't good enough to edge them, so this delivery was wasted on a good umpire. Ultimately it looked a howler from Mervyn Kitchen, but there was no way he could have given it out with a clear conscience on first viewing – or, probably, even second or third.

It might have been the ultimate example of reverse swing, probably the most important and surely the most thrilling of all cricket's many innovations. Wasim bowled many more famous deliveries and spells – notably the over that effectively won the 1992 World Cup final against England, and a legendary working-over of Rahul Dravid in the Chennai Test of 1998–99 – but this was arguably the most difficult to comprehend.

The apogee of reverse swing came four years earlier, first when Pakistan won the World Cup and then when Wasim and Waqar Younis inflicted all manner of collapses on England in a scorching five-Test series: nine for 102 and eight for 67 at Lord's; eight for 28 at Headingley; and seven for 25 at the Oval. Pakistan won 2–1 and most of England, tediously, cried foul.

It soon became clear that reverse swing was a gift for which we should all be thankful. Hand in hand with the legspin renaissance, it revitalised the game in the nineties. We cannot be entirely sure of its origins, beyond the fact that it was developed in Pakistan, possibly as far back as the Second World War, as a response to parched pitches. A little further down, its lineage is clearer: it was patented by Imran Khan and by Sarfraz Nawaz, who boomeranged the ball to such an extent against Australia at Melbourne in 1978–79 that he took 7 wickets for 1 run as part of overall figures of 9 for 86. Imran also credits the Australian Max Walker, but the art was first truly mastered by Wasim and Waqar, who notably ran amok in England in 1992.

Cricket's response to such an unknown science was first fear (allegations of ball-tampering), then ignorance (the dirt-in-the-pocket affair involving Mike Atherton). But as time has gone on it has become appreciated for the minor miracle it is, and more has been understood about the mechanics: pace and full length are prerequisites, as is a fast arm and, ideally, a relative lack of height, although that didn't stop Andrew Flintoff bamboozling the Australians during the 2005 Ashes. A bone dry outfield is also of help. As the name suggests, it reverses the norms of orthodox swing bowling: while one side of the ball is kept shiny, the other must be made as dry and rough as possible, which is why the old ball became such a deadly weapon: against Pakistan in the nineties, opening batsmen were in the peculiar position of trying to cash in against the new ball.

Reverse swing has also enabled bowlers to be entirely self-sufficient, needing no help from pitch of umpire, height not being an issue in LBWs that result from reverse swing. Both Wasim and Waqar took more than half their Test wickets through bowleds and LBWs. Ultimately, reverse swing has meant more collapses, more hat-tricks and, as the *Wisden Cricketers' Almanack* editor Scyld Berry pointed out, more results: tailenders are simply not equipped to handle a ball boomeranging in at their toes. Ask Robert Croft.

England (326 & 242) lost to Pakistan (521-8 dec & 48-1) by nine wickets

Cricketers have always shown an endearing willingness to share the mystery of their innovation; to put the game above parochial concerns. When Arthur Mailey was told by a teammate that showing a secret grip to an English opponent was not in Australia's best interests, he said simply: 'Art is universal.' Another Aussie, Dennis Lillee, has had a profound impact on pace-bowling resources around the world, but particularly in India, through his work at the MRF Pace Foundation. Lillee himself was taught the leg-cutter by John Snow. The reverse swing of Andrew Flintoff and Simon Jones that so thrillingly befuddled Australia in 2005 was partly learned through working with Wasim Akram and Waqar Younis at Lancashire and Glamorgan respectively. And on Australia's tour of Pakistan in 1994–95, the two great legspinners of modern times, Abdul Qadir and Shane Warne, discussed their art in Qadir's house, an almost impossibly romantic scene.

Warne also took time to give a televised tutorial to two young English legspinners, Sussex's Will Beer and Somerset's Max Waller, during the lunch interval on the final day of the 2009 Ashes. Four years earlier, during a routine thrashing of Bangladesh by England at Durham, Steve Harmison sat on the balcony giving tips on wrist position to Bangladesh's young seamers. (This was not a Machiavellian plot; at that stage Harmison's radar was more Shaun Pollock than Jackson Pollock.)

THE MRF PACE FOUNDATION IS FORMED
AUGUST 1987

The 2007–08 Test series between Australia and India was so fractious that an important facet of India's victory at Perth was lost. It was that *India won at Perth*. Short of a couple of legspinners bowling England to victory on a Mumbai turner, it is impossible to imagine a more unlikely or symbolic victory. Subcontinental sides had previous lost all nine Tests on the WACA trampoline, most by enormous margins, but now India's fast bowlers outdid Australia's.

It was, irony of ironies, a victory largely made in Australia. Dennis Lillee, a man with arguably the finest fast-bowling brain of them all, had been working at the MRF Pace Foundation in Chennai for two decades, and this was the ultimate reward for his work. There is no finer example of how cricket's desire to share skills transcends parochalism; indeed, while Lillee's work is predominantly with Indians, the likes of Glenn McGrath and Chaminda Vaas spent time at the MRF in their formative years.

Lillee, who spends a few weeks a year in Chennai, took the job for the challenge, and the love of the game. 'Australia's always produced fast bowlers,' he said. 'India never has, and there was this myth that Indians couldn't really bowl fast. Seemed interesting to see if I couldn't help bust that bubble.' For the rest of the year it is run by T. A. Sekar, who played two Tests in the 1980s and was probably the fastest Indian bowler of his generation.

Sekar and Lillee have been on board since the MRF was founded in 1987; with their forensic understanding of fast bowling, the flexibility to treat no two bowlers the same and facilities that are the envy of the world, it quickly became a byword for excellence. If not quite the BBC or HBO, this is still an acronym you can implicitly trust.

Lillee was the key signing, but the MRF only became possible because of the remarkable ambition of the late Ravi Mammen. At a time when Kapil Dev was India's only top-class fast bowler, Mammen dreamed of a day when a phalanx of Indian bowlers could bowl genuinely fast. That seemed impossible, like changing the DNA of a nation, but Mammen funded his dream and, while he passed away in 1990, it at last came to full fruition on those five glorious days at Perth.

If the wilful sharing of secrets shows cricket's capacity to cross continents, then it can also cross generations. The sight of a fine, apparently fading player enjoying a late flowering is a delicious evocation of the spirit of cricket. Examples include Angus Fraser in the Caribbean in 1997–98, when he took 20 wickets in the first two Tests after an unexpected recall, and Cyril Washbrook in 1956. Washbrook, an England selector who was aged 41 and had not played Test cricket for five years, was asked to leave the room during a selection meeting; when he returned he was informed that his fellow selectors wanted to pick him for the third Test against Australia at Headingley after England had been thrashed in the second Test at Lord's. *Wisden* said that 'the decision was greeted first with astonishment and then with delight.' Washbrook arrived at the crease with England in a mess at 17-3, but made a patient 98 to set up an innings victory. He played the remainder of the series before leaving the Test scene again, this time for good.

The intrinsic charm of improbable success is magnified in other areas, particularly when a batsman or bowler excels in the other discpline. The look on occasional offspinner Michael Vaughan's face when he bowled Sachin Tendulkar through the gate at Trent Bridge in 2002 lingers, as do the celebrations when Glenn McGrath – a man who did not even reach double figures until his 22nd Test – made his maiden Test half-century in his 102nd match, against New Zealand in 2004–05. For a bowler, a maiden century (or half-century in the case of those with realistically limited ambitions like McGrath) is the sporting equivalent of a man's dying wish. Derek Underwood (at first-class level), Chaminda Vaas and Anil Kumble (both at Test level) all reached three figures for the first time in their dotage. The greats can even surprise themselves within their own discipline. In his extraordinary psychological dismantling of England at Adelaide in 2006, Shane Warne even bowled Matthew Hoggard with the googly, a delivery he never mastered and rarely bowled. It was Warne's 694th Test wicket, yet he had the childlike glee of a kid who had just taken his first.

Sydney Copley and Gary Pratt never took a Test wicket or scored a run, yet they have a place in Test history because of famous contributions as substitutes. Pratt ran Ricky Ponting out in the fourth Ashes Test of 2005, perhaps the moment the series flipped decisively towards England, and was such a part of England's celebrations that he got everything but the MBE. Copley's 15 yards of fame belonged to more sober times, but he took a match-winning catch in the first Ashes Test of 1930.

SYDNEY COPLEY
ENGLAND V AUSTRALIA, 1ST TEST, TRENT BRIDGE, 13–17 JUNE 1930

It may not have changed his life as it did Gary Pratt's, but Sydney Copley's contribution as substitute was every bit as unexpectedly charming and integral to an England Ashes victory at Trent Bridge as Pratt's was in 2005. Not that you would know it from a flick through *Wisden*. Until recently, all substitute catches and run-outs did not credit the fielder involved. So whereas the scorecard for the Trent Bridge Test of 2005 reads 'Ponting run out (sub [GJ Pratt]) 48', its equivalent for the Trent Bridge Test of 1930 says simply 'McCabe c sub b Tate 49'. Never mind the cover; some books should not be judged by their content either.

Copley, a 24-year-old on the Nottinghamshire groundstaff who had never played first-class cricket, was called on as substitute in place of the injured Harold Larwood on the fourth day with Australia chasing an unlikely target of 429. It was typical of Jack Hobbs that he should put him at ease with what Copley described as a 'few kind words'. With Australia on 267-4, Copley's 15 yards of fame arrived. The brilliant Stan McCabe, who had moved fluently to 49, pulled Maurice Tate towards mid-on, and Copley took an outstanding diving catch on the run, keeping hold of the ball despite an involuntary somersault.

England cruised to victory thereafter to take a 1–0 series lead, although a Bradman-fuelled Australia came back to win 2–1. Copley made his first-class debut the following week, against Oxford University, but it was also his last game.

England (270 & 302) beat Australia (144 & 335) by 93 runs

Neither Copley or Pratt would live up to their promise as batsmen, yet the seductive infinity of potential continues to enthral. Cricket is rarely more romantic, the spirit rarely more alive, than when a young player signals his arrival on the big stage. Frequently the reality does not live up to the fantasy of that breakthrough performance – scarcity is important for greatness to matter – yet, like the joyous first weeks of an ultimately doomed relationship, the memories burn bright.

Englishman of a certain age have never seen any innings infused with such hope and happiness as that played by 19-year-old Ben Hollioake on his debut against Australia at Lord's in 1997, a carefree 48-ball 63 that included the most insouciant six off Shane Warne. This is not dreamy revisionism in response to Hollioake's tragically premature death in 2002 ; it was in evidence at the time, in the members 'rising creakily from their benches to acclaim him', as Tim de Lisle put it, or in the excitable chatter up and down the country about a performance that was unprecedented for *any* Englishman on debut, never mind a 19-year-old playing against the best team in the world. 'He stays, in cricket's folk memory, forever young,' said de Lisle, 'and when you think of him, you think of that day at Lord's.'

At the end of 2009, 86 players had made centuries on debuts, from Australia's Charles Bannerman in the very first Test to the West Indies' Adrian Barath in Test number 1,936. Which linger in your memory? Mark Waugh's angelic 138 against England at Adelaide in 1990–91 might be one; in *Wisden Cricket Monthly* the innings was described as being 'so sublime that sages battled to recall a better start to a Test career'. As for the bowlers, we might recall the Trueman Show, when Fred Trueman marked his debut by taking three quick wickets as India were reduced to 0-4 at Headingley in 1952, still the worst start to an innings in Test history. And it is a measure of how well England played to win in India in 1984–85 that they did so despite startling performances from two nascent talents, Mohammad Azharrudin and Laxman Sivaramakrishnan. Azharrudin, in his debut series, made impossibly charming hundreds in three consecutive Tests, while Sivaramakrishnan took six-fors in three consecutive innings. Sivaramakrishnan had played a solitary Test 18 months earlier, showing that it does not have to be a player's debut for the breakthrough to linger; often it is even more memorable if he has struggled before, as with Inzamam-ul-Haq at the 1992 World Cup.

INZAMAM-UL-HAQ
NEW ZEALAND V PAKISTAN, WORLD CUP SEMI-FINAL, AUCKLAND, 21 MARCH 1992

With his hangdog gait and run of low scores, Inzamam was a soft touch at his first World Cup. He made just 123 runs from eight innings in the group stages, but his captain Imran Khan knew he had a special talent on his hands, and Inzy finally proved it in the semi-final against the co-hosts New Zealand.

When he came to the crease Pakistan needed 123 for 15 overs – a huge task in those days – and were being squeezed to death by New Zealand's phalanx of dobbers. It was turning into one big carnival of Kiwi cricket, but Inzamam, like a lumbering friendly bear inadvertently wreaking havoc at a circus, demolished one attraction after another. Chris Harris was hoicked brutally for four and then driven dreamily over long-off for a slow-motion, will-it-won't-it six; Gavin Larsen was flayed through the covers; and Dipak Patel, the secret weapon, was pulled savagely for two fours in one over.

Inzamam, fleet of foot and foppish of appearance back then, roared to a stunning 60 from 37 balls before being run out, but he had set Pakistan up for victory – and he showed that he could repeat the dose with another assault on England in the final. These were no fifteen minutes of fame; a special talent had arrived, and fifteen years later he would still be punishing hapless bowlers.
New Zealand (262-7) lost to Pakistan (264-6) by four wickets

Inzamam has never been the most svelte of his characters, and cricket has invariably found a place for the less athletic type, prioritising talent over fitness. Even now, in an age of ice baths and exercise scientists, there are a few players fighting the unhealthy fight: Ramesh Powar and Darren Lehmann, for instance. Warwick Armstong, the great Australian captain who was known as The Big Ship, frequently weighed in at over 20 stone. And when Bermuda's left-arm spinner Dwayne Leverock, all 20 stone of him, took a flying slip catch against India, it was one of the moments of the 2007 World Cup. The previous World Cup, in South Africa in 2003, showed that losing weight isn't always beneficial: in a pre-tournament diet, Inzamam lost almost as many kilos (17) as he would make runs in South Africa (19 in six innings).

Inzamam was dropped after that, although within six months he would be not only back in the team but also the captain. The role of the cricket captain is like no other in sport. He must be tactician, figurehead, father figure and detached superior, and he must legitimise all of the above by performing with bat or ball.

MARK NICHOLAS

When I was privileged to sit down in a small committee with Colin Cowdrey and then latterly Ted Dexter to discuss the Spirit of Cricket Preamble, the key word was respect: respect to your opponent, to yourself and to the game, and we felt that if you showed those you would almost certainly adhere to the spirit of cricket.

Cricket is an unlimiting sport. It's available to everybody of every size and shape and style. It doesn't bracket you or box you. It's unique in allowing you to be who you are, and allowing your talent to be whatever it may be. You simply need to have an ability to relate your skill to the task at hand, and the spirit of the game is that it will allow your talent to flourish if you use it competently and, above all, with enthusiasm. It's extraordinary, for example, that you could be a successful cricketer by being on the field all day and doing absolutely nothing apart from taking a catch five minutes before the close that changes a game. Or you could bat for an hour for nought, but you might be in a partnership of 70 that wins a match.

To demonstrate the way cricket embraces all types, there are three characters from an era of English cricket that I grew up in and learnt about. You had the bespectacled Geoff Boycott, who could do nothing else but bat – nothing else – but he could block, he could keep the opposition out, and he has become an English cult hero. You had the lanky, unlikely Bob Willis, who had an odd, goose-like run-up and wasn't an elegant, natural cricketer, but who fulfilled his role because he could bowl a cricket ball extremely fast. Also in the same team you had the utterly quirky, some would say completely dotty, wicketkeeper Alan Knott.

All three of those human beings, so utterly different in every way as people, played in the same team in totally different roles and were equally important as one another in fields that bore no relation to each other.

Mark Nicholas played for Hampshire between 1978 and 1995, scoring 18,262 first-class runs at 34.39. He also captained England A. He is now a cricket commentator for Five in England and Nine in Australia.

The captain's greatest gift to the spirit of the game might be his ability to impose a doctrine of attacking cricket. This can be a double-edged sword, as two of the great attacking captains, Steve

Waugh and Sir Garfield Sobers, would testify. There reigns are perhaps best remembered for spectacular defeats, at Kolkata and Trinidad respectively; in reality, such defeats could almost be lauded, as they were largely the consequence of a remorselessly attacking philosophy.

STEVE WAUGH TAKES OVER AS AUSTRALIAN TEST CAPTAIN
12 FEBRUARY 1999

In the 20th century, Test cricket was not a frivolous business. There were unspoken rules about how the game should be played: cautiously, and with respect. There were ways to behave. You could let your hair down when you played one-day cricket.

And then Steve Waugh asked why. When he succeeded Mark Taylor in 1999, Waugh took attacking captaincy to an almost unimaginable level and completed a perfect trilogy of Australian captaincy that took them from their mid-eighties doldrums to one of the greatest teams in the game's history. Under Border they stopped losing; under Taylor they started to win more often than not; under Waugh they began to marmalise teams.

If Mark Taylor subtly attempted to abolish the draw, Waugh openly abhorred it. Of his 57 Tests as captain, Australia drew only seven and only two of those were not rain-affected. Waugh's most famous commandment was that his side should score 300 runs in a day, although ironically, in his first innings as Australian Test captain, they managed only 174-6 from 90 overs on the first day. Overall they scored only 269 from 121.3 overs in that innings, a funereal 2.21 per over, with Glenn McGrath of all people the only man to score at more than 50 runs per 100 balls.

Yet there was more to it than scoring runs. Waugh strived to put opposing teams under the fiercest pressure at every point of a match. He challenged every accepted norm of captaincy and often came up with a successful alternative. For example, he would often win the toss and bowl first – a practice that was previously about as acceptable in Australia as swigging a warm beer – because he figured that the sooner the opposition were batting, the sooner Australia could start taking those 20 wickets they needed for victory. Waugh won the toss 31 times as Australian Test captain; on the 11 occasions that he bowled first, Australia won 11 times. He would frequently declare unexpectedly 10 or 15 overs before the close, desperate to get a wicket before stumps. Invariably he'd get two. He also put the concept of the nightwatchman to sleep.

Waugh, of course, was blessed with an unbelievably gifted side, yet in no sense was he covering his own back. By investing everything in pursuit of victory, he left himself open to defeat, as famously happened in India in 2000–01, when India followed on 274 behind and won thanks to V. V. S. Laxman's legendary 281. Other captains would have closed that game out for a draw, but Waugh insisted on pursuing victory regardless of the consequences.

Australia went on to lose one of the great series, 2–1. Ostensibly this tarnished Waugh's legacy, yet the manner of it deserved to reinforce his place as the father of all attacking captains – especially when, as the 21st century took shape, his approach was copied worldwide. Three hundred runs in a day became the norm; the Test-match draw became an endangered species; and even England, who Waugh criticised in 2000 for taking part in the 'most boring series he'd ever seen' against Pakistan, began to buckle their swash.

When England turned the 2005 Ashes on its head by scoring an incredible 407 in only 79.2 overs on the first day at Edgbaston – the second-highest scoring rate in a completed innings in Test history – Waugh might even have allowed himself a little smile. As teams considered their tactics for a Test match, they no longer asked 'why?' Because of Waugh, they asked 'why not?'

Steve Waugh's record as Australian Test captain was P57 W41 D7 L9

There is also a huge charm to the notion of the specialist captain. Harry Trott, who led Australia at the end of the 19th century, was not exactly a specialist skipper but he was probably the first great captain, a man who revolutionised the role through his incessant shuffling of fielders and bowlers at a time when both were done formulaically. Probably the most famous captain of all is Mike Brearley, who averaged 22.88 from 39 Tests yet is widely recognised as England's greatest-ever leader, the man whom the Australian fast bowler Rodney Hogg said had a 'degree in people'. His book, *The Art of Captaincy*, was even cited by Sam Mendes as a regular source of inspiration during his Oscar-winning directorship of *American Beauty*. In the 1984 Benson & Hedges Trophy final, Lancashire's captain John Abrahams received the Man of the Match award, even though he was out for nought and did not bowl.

JOHN ABRAHAMS
LANCASHIRE V WARWICKSHIRE, BENSON & HEDGES CUP FINAL, LORD'S, 21 JULY 1984

There was no obvious candidate for Man of the Match when Lancashire won the Benson & Hedges Cup final of 1984. It might have gone to either of their opening bowlers, Paul Allott and Steve Jefferies, who each took three wickets; or to a 20-year-old Neil Fairbrother, who top-scored for Lancashire with a chipper unbeaten 36 that hinted at the special talent we would later see with England; or to Alvin Kallicharran, whose brave 70 in treacherous batting conditions comprised more than half Warwickshire's total.

Instead, the adjudicator Peter May gave it to the Lancashire captain John Abrahams, who had not bowled and scored a duck. May said that Abrahams got the award for 'his overall control of the team', although the losing captain Bob Willis had a different take: 'I suppose he got it for winning the toss.'

'This seemed an emotional rather than hard-headed choice,' said Paul Fitzpatrick in the *Guardian*. 'Abrahams was more surprised than anyone, but it could not have gone to a nicer cricketer and it was no bad thing to see an adjudicator coming up with something original.'

Warwickshire (139) lost to Lancashire (140-4) by 6 wickets

Such modest contributions have not always been tolerated, however. Around the turn of the century, Mark Taylor and Nasser Hussain – erudite, streetwise captains leading Australia and England into new territory – came under asphyxiating media pressure because of a lack of runs. Their redemptive centuries, at Edgbaston and Kandy in 1997 and 2001 respectively, were two of the more rewarding innings of modern times. In that same series, Taylor made one of the great captaincy decisions when, with Australia 1–0 down in the Ashes, he bravely batted first on a wet Old Trafford wicket, relatively secure in the knowledge that Shane Warne would have a big impact in the fourth innings. After a torrid start, Australia – inspired by Warne – won at a canter.

DAVID LLOYD

I played in a successful young Lancashire side, and for me this was a defining moment in terms of the way the game was played. Lancashire were playing Nottinghamshire at Old Trafford in the early seventies, Peter Lever was the bowler and there was a massive appeal against Basharat Hassan. The umpire, Eddie Phillipson, gave him out, and Basharat made an almighty song and dance on the way off.

He got to the gate and then our captain Jack Bond brought him back. He said, 'Look Eddie I don't think he's hit it.' Now we had no say in that; it was our leader, who felt that there had been a wrong. If he made a decision, that was it. He decided our direction. He was a great influence on so many people, in character and spirit. For my money he is the best advert for Lancashire cricket that there's ever been.

He moulded characters; he moulded *your* character. He was easily the biggest influence of my life really. He got a young team together and made us into a very good side, but also he moulded us in terms of how you play. For example, he told us, if you don't walk you don't play. He was much older than most of us - 15 years my senior, 12 years Clive Lloyd's - and we all had total respect for the bloke. We were tough - flippin' heck, there were some tough boys in that team - but the ethics and the spirit of the game were ingrained in you at a very early age. In my opinion Jack Bond took it a stage further because his leadership was so strong. We all followed him. When he called Basharat back, nobody even thought to query it.

David Lloyd, Lancashire 1965–83, England 1974–75

Jack Bond was Lancashire captain from 1968 to 1972, when they won the first two Sunday Leagues and three consecutive Gillette Cups.

The influence of a captain such as Taylor inevitably extends beyond the pitch. The likes of Imran Khan, Arjuna Ranatunga and Frank Worrell also possessed such an aura and a wisdom that would have an impact on the lives of their young charges. Never mind the umpire; the captain's word was also final. As with the game itself, the spirit of cricket is understood both individually and collectively.

GRAEME SMITH

To me, the spirit of cricket is about how you represent the game. Obviously behaviour on and off the field is crucial, but it is also about trying to do justice to the ability you've been given. The best way for me to do that is to ensure that I give my best in every facet of the game; that applies equally whether I'm at a match, a training session or even a function.

Initially, when I was given the captaincy at 22, I was pretty single-minded about trying to make a success of my career, but along the way a number of things, both good and bad, opened my eyes to what the game is all about. One example was when I batted with a broken hand at Sydney in 2009. I honestly had no idea of the impact that innings would have. But it really made me aware of the influence we have on people's lives, and that it goes far beyond the hundreds you score, the wickets you take and the games you win. We're representing something much greater.

When I was growing up, two people I really respected were Steve Waugh and Gary Kirsten. Gary gave me lots of really good advice. The best bit was, '"Learn your strengths and weaknesses as a cricketer and a person as quickly as you can".' I had to be true to myself, and that's how I thought I could be successful in my career and respect the spirit of the game.

Graeme Smith, South Africa 2002–

CHAPTER THREE

The poor souls who graze at third man or fine leg for six hours a day might disagree, but no cricketer is an island. Or, as the former England all-rounder Ronnie Irani put it rather more earthily: 'There's no I in team but there is an I in winner.' Individual contributions to the spirit of cricket are invariably if not inextricably linked to the team context. One of cricket's principal charms is the tantalising and unique way in which it fuses individual and team sports. Such a concept might seem absurd, and invite memory of *The Office*'s David Brent and his daft philosophy of 'team individuality', yet in cricket it somehow *does* work that way. As Rahul Bhattacharya says: 'Cricket is only nominally a team sport. It is cumulative rather than collaborative. Each delivery is an isolated event, a classic one-on-one duel.' Yet the collective achievement is ultimately all that counts, hence Simon Barnes's marvellous description of the run-hungry Kevin Pietersen as a 'team egomaniac'.

ROBERT KEY

Cricket has always prided itself on its conduct, and its gentlemanly play, and I think Freddie's handshake with Brett Lee at Edgbaston in 2005 took that to another level. Incidents like that are why cricket can hold its head up high compared to other sports. That's the way Freddie is. He plays cricket just for the sheer enjoyment of it. Whatever happens he can have a smile on his face, and he'll go up and shake the hand of the bloke whose head he's been trying to knock off for the last hour. He appreciates what they've done, and he has a respect and a love for the game.

The fact you can have such an individual duel within a team sport is what makes the game so interesting. You can hide sometimes in other team sports, but in cricket you can blatantly be the person who has cost your side the game. The fact that there is not much going on between each ball magnifies the action when it happens. There is also the fact that a match will often last five days: it's not just 80 or 90 minutes; it's four or five days of hard slog. You get to drinks in the first session of a Test match and you've almost played three-quarters of a football game. I think that's why there's that appreciation of what your opponent has to go through during a match - not so much physically as mentally. Cricket is an individual sport within a team game, which is almost unique.

Robert Key, England 2002–

The rhythm of a first-class match, spread over four innings and up to five days, is a joy. It is hard to imagine a more compelling sporting format: an art-house subtlety runs throughout, with intermittent blockbuster scenes which somehow do not undermine the narrative. The notion of the five-day draw is seen by some, especially in America, as one of cricket's premier weaknesses; in fact it is something to be cherished. There is no doubt that some draws can be spectacularly tedious, but that is the case in all sports: what is unique to cricket is the narrative complexity of the more interesting draws, as shown on England's tour of South Africa in 2009–10, when the last man Graham Onions twice survived the final over to secure a draw.

The fact that scores frequently range from around 100 to 600 – and occasionally higher or lower – allows for so many different stories. Especially prominent are the high-scoring shootout – a guaranteed crowd-draw in the 20th century, but not with the increased scoring rates of the last ten years – the low-scoring dogfight and those marvellous contests when the scores are like a mathematical puzzle (281, 321, 274, ???) and nobody knows who has the ascendancy until the final session. One of the great examples occurred in Barbados in 1987–88, when Pakistan's 309 and 262 played West Indies' 306 and 268-8 (from 207-8). In winning the match, West Indies maintained their long unbeaten run in Test series. There were 18 scores in excess of 30 yet nobody passed 67. It might just be the perfect Test. There can be significant crossover too, as any England fan still traumatised by Adelaide 2006 will tell you. England scored

551-6 declared in their first innings, but still contrived to lose by six wickets after being dismissed for 129 second time round on an unforgettable final day.

That collapse killed a promising series stone dead, but there have been umpteen other series – especially those of four and five Tests – that have ebbed and flowed thrillingly. 'A series of more than three Tests is a rare thing these days,' wrote Rahul Bhattacharya in 2003. 'Its shifting dynamics embrace such abstractions as momentum, luck, form, intensity – karma, even – as if it were a universe in itself. India's tour of England in 2002 captured the ebb and flow, the up and down, of this strange and enchanting realm.' Such enchantment can be in evidence in a three-Test series: consecutive 1–1 draws between the West Indies and Pakistan in 1986–87, 1988 and 1990–91 were of a staggeringly high quality.

The vagaries of pitch conditions also add a layer of intrigue. They can allow David to topple Goliath; the otherwise omnipotent West Indies side of the eighties and early nineties had a peculiar penchant for farcical collapses against often modest spin bowling. At Sydney in 1984–85, Murray Bennett and Bob Holland shared 15 wickets in an improbable Australian triumph; in the rest of their career, they took just 25 wickets between them in 12 Tests. On the same ground four years later, Allan Border bagged 11 wickets in an equally unexpected victory, having gone into the match with 16 wickets from 100 Tests. Similarly, a seaming monster of a pitch can make an ogre of an otherwise workaday bowler. England have had umpteen horses for the

Headingley course, few as successful than Neil Mallender, who bowled Pakistan to defeat with eight wickets on debut in 1992 but only played one more Test, his limitations at the highest level painfully exposed in less favourable conditions.

Different conditions also offers scope for the distinction between flat-track bullies and rough-track maestros such as Jack Hobbs, Garry Sobers – whose unbeaten 113 on a badly cracked Sabina Park track against England in 1967–68 might be the greatest bad-wicket innings every played – and Victor Trumper.

Hobbs, Sobers and Trumper all abhorred the superfluous run and relished the chance to play innings that really mattered. It would be remiss to ignore the fact that some batsmen care only for the quantitative value of the runs; the desire for the red ink of 'not out' has become a black mark against plenty of careers. This is far from a contemporary problem. In 1910, after the MCC announced that, as a response to self-indulgent batting, only wins would count in the County Championship, the *Manchester Guardian* bemoaned 'the rut of averages and other destroying immoralities that have submerged the real spirit of cricket'.

The flip side of that is that the spirit of cricket is rarely more alive than when a batsman performs with little or no regard for his average. This may seem like an obvious moral responsibility, but it is more complicated than that, especially if you are playing for your place in the knowledge that selectors can be as liable as the public to judge you on the very average that you are supposed to disregard for the greater good.

BRIAN CLOSE
ENGLAND V AUSTRALIA, 4TH TEST, OLD TRAFFORD,
27 JULY–1 AUGUST 1961

Brian Close had more reason than most to bat for himself. His England career spanned more years (27) than matches (22); and incredibly, his first eight Test caps came in seven different series. It redefined impermanence. All of which makes his always unselfish, team-oriented batting even more admirable, with one particular example leaping out.

When Richie Benaud famously went around the wicket to bowl Australia to a dramatic and Ashes-winning victory over England at Old Trafford in 1961, Close was slaughtered for his dismissal, when he top-edged a sweep to Norm O'Neill at backward square leg. Even though this was his first Test back in the side, he was immediately dropped. It would become one of the most reviled shots in English cricket history, up there with Mike Gatting's reverse-sweep in the 1987 World Cup final. *The Times* said the shot was 'best talked about in whispers' and that Close batted 'as if out of his cricketing senses'.

The truth was the exact opposite. Close was entirely in control of his senses and, unlike his teammates, came up with a bespoke plan to deal with Benaud's increasing threat and to maintain England's slim chance of victory. In his autobiography he devotes an entire chapter to detailing his thought processes; it has almost as many pages (seven) as the innings lasted in minutes (eight).

It was typical Close. While many were content to be *seen* to be doing the right thing, Close simply wanted to *do* the right thing for his team. It is about the little things that go unseen that only you know you have done.

Close was an extraordinarily selfless batsman. It was not only conscience that made him this way; he also had the keenest of cricketing brains, which would come up with a plan dependent on the precise circumstances of the contest. As his Cricinfo profile says: 'Because he always tried to play the type of innings he considered the position of the match required, Close's record did scant justice to his talent, which was huge.'

He may have failed against Australia, but there can be few greater examples of selflessness than a young man placing his international career in jeopardy not only for the good of his team, but in the pursuit of victory to the exclusion of everything else.

Australia (190 & 432) beat England (367 & 201) by 54 runs

The West Indian all-rounder Learie Constantine averaged 19 with the bat and 30 with the ball in Tests, figures that tell nothing of the lustrous entertainment he provided. And in the modern era, it seemed nicely appropriate that, after 11 years in which the quality of his contribution far exceeded the statistical achievement, Andrew Flintoff should sign off from Test cricket with a match-changing contribution that would not even be recorded in his statistics, the run out of Ricky Ponting at The Oval.

In the December 1996 edition of *Wisden Cricket Monthly*, Scyld Berry argued that batsmen should be judged not by averages but by the number of initiatives seized for their side.

The two recurring names in the piece were those of Michael Slater, Australia's joyously carefree opener, and Graham Thorpe. Thorpe is often remembered as the crotchety nurdler of his dotage, but at his best he was a marvellous counter-attacker who frequently took bowlers on as soon as he came to the crease – no mean feat given the quality of fast bowling in the nineties, the fact that his place was not at all secure for the first couple of years of his Test career, and the fact that England would invariably be behind in the match. Crunch-time after crunch-time he would punch England back into contention by copying a trick Steve Waugh patented: get to 20 or 30 at a run a ball, spread the field, release the pressure, and then knuckle down to play an orthodox innings.

MICHAEL SLATER HITS PHIL DEFREITAS FOR FOUR
AUSTRALIA V ENGLAND, 1ST TEST, BRISBANE, 25-29 NOVEMBER 1994

Phil DeFreitas took 140 Test wickets. He was part of an Ashes-winning team at the age of 20. Between 1991 and 1994 he was England's best fast bowler. He won a Test at Adelaide in 1995 with a glorious counter-attacking 88. He even had a trademark comic grimace every time he bowled that made him look like a man in the throes of a painful orgasm.

None of these define DeFreitas's career. Instead, harsh though it is, he is remembered as the man who lost the Ashes after one ball. That was in the first Test at Brisbane in 1994–95. England had travelled Down Under with genuine optimism after a thrilling drawn series against South Africa (who had themselves drawn home and away against Australia the previous winter). It didn't take long for their hopes to unravel. DeFreitas kicked off the series with a nervous long hop that was crashed witheringly for four by Michael Slater. It was a bad ball, but no worse than most looseners. Any other batsmen in the world would have watched the delivery go past their off stump. That's what opening batsmen did. But Slater was different.

The last ball of the over suffered the same treatment. The tone of Australian hegemony was set, and they romped to 329 for four at the close – standard fare these days, but revelatory at the time; only five years earlier they had closed the first day of the Ashes series on 207 for three – and eventually to a 3–1 victory. It was one that most had safely predicted after the very first ball.

MICHAEL SLATER

In this age of power batting it is usual to see openers smack the new ball to all parts in Test cricket. Back then, little more than a decade ago, it was as inappropriate as bassoons in dance music. Openers did attrition; Slater did aggression. Openers eschewed risk; Slater calculated risk. Every time he strapped on the pads he also buckled his swash.

Bopping around his crease on the balls of his feet, he would land savage blow after savage blow with his bullet cut shots, cover-drives and pings through midwicket. And in a team full of champions whose brilliance and braggadocio provoked such misplaced distaste, Slater was the token good cop, an infectious bundle of hyperactivity you just couldn't dislike. He lived fast and died young, with his Test career over at the age of 31 just as his peers, such as Langer, Matthew Hayden, Damien Martyn and Adam Gilchrist, were warming up.

Unlike most great punishers, such as Viv Richards and Hayden, Slater's threat was not physical, it was psychological. He gave bowlers the fear and made their chief weapon, the new ball, something to be dreaded rather than relished. In Mark Taylor's Australian side he was the chief enforcer; the fact that 11 of his 14 centuries came in victory, and none in defeat, spoke volumes about his importance.

Slater and Thorpe excelled against fast bowlers, yet the most obvious example of selfless batting is the calculated assault against a potentially dangerous spinner who is settling in for a long spell. Jack Hobbs would frequently take on Charlie Parker, one of the great left-arm spinners, on turning wickets. 'I have seen him hit Charlie over the top of extra cover or mid-off four or five times in a couple of overs and drive him off,' said Tom Goddard, the Gloucestershire off-spinner who formed a lethal spin duo with Parker, at least when Hobbs wasn't around. 'Then, for the next hour or two, Charlie was fielding at third man when he should have been bowling Surrey out.'

On England's tour of India in 1992–93, the eccentric Navjot Sidhu identified the 40-year-old offspinner John Emburey as England's main slow-bowling asset and launched an extended assault of such ferocity that Emburey, one of the game's great cussers, probably formulated new swearwords in response. Sidhu drove Emburey for nine sixes in two warm-up games: the majority were straight-driven, the ultimate demonstration of a batsman's effortless supremacy over a spinner. It so damaged Emburey's confidence that England left him out of the first Test, preferring Ian Salisbury, who a) wasn't even in the original tour party and b) was Ian Salisbury. When Emburey returned for the third and final Test, Sidhu slapped him for another.

Such an approach carries significant risk, given the inevitable opprobrium should it go wrong. Ian Botham was one of the great selfless batsmen, always at his happiest when he was giving it some humpty and seizing the initiative. But inevitably this could not always come off, and few will forget his laughable dismissal against Australia at Old Trafford in 1989. Botham was still on 0 when he charged the legspinner Trevor Hohns, and tried to deposit him somewhere over the Pennines. Botham missed by a mile and was bowled, a split-second before he would have been stumped when halfway down the pitch.

Then there is the case of Martin Crowe, New Zealand's greatest-ever batsman, who gambled and lost against England in Christchurch in 1991–92. With New Zealand nine down in their second innings, and with the time/runs equation at its absolute limit – there were ten minutes to go – Crowe knew that, with the field brought in to save every run, if he hit Phil Tufnell for four the match would be drawn, but that if he was dismissed the match would be lost. Crowe tried to go over the top and skied to mid-off. To risk such ignominy for the greater good is surely the sign of a batsman in tune with the spirit of the game.

The inherent contradiction in our understanding of what constitutes that spirit is reflected by the fact that a number of other famous premeditated assaults came from Hansie Cronje, hardly a man with whom the concept is associated. Yet before he was disgraced, Cronje was masterful in this area: he contemptuously hit the recalled Ian Salisbury out of the fourth Test at Trent Bridge in 1998, and earlier in the year played a gem of an innings against a rampant Muttiah Muralitharan. South Africa, 1–0 up in the series, were chasing 226 to win the final Test, but had slipped from 89–0 to 99–3, with all three wickets going to Murali on a wearing pitch. South Africa were simply intent on survival, letting Murali bowl at them, but Cronje turned that on its head with a startling assault. He hit Murali for four and six immediately and eventually moved to 50 off just 31 balls – at that stage the second-fastest in Test history – reaching it by hitting Murali for three consecutive sixes. Cronje finished with 82 from 63 balls, a performance of stunning audacity, and South Africa won by six wickets.

Our understanding of selfless batting tends to involve attacks of that nature, given their inherent risk, but it can work both ways: it is equally rewarding to watch a naturally attacking batsman fight desperately against his basic instincts for the sake of the team. Viv Richards poetically recalled how he 'watched the ball until my eyes hurt' during a matchwinning century for Somerset against Warwickshire in the Gillette Cup in 1978. At The Oval in 1956, in his final Ashes innings, Australia's bombastic allrounder Keith Miller denied his basic instinct to make an unbeaten 7 in nearly 25 overs to spare Australia a humiliating defeat against Jim Laker and Tony Lock.

On the same ground 31 years later, Botham made 51 from 209 balls to save a Test against Pakistan, all the while resisting the teasing flight of their spin duo Abdul Qadir and Tauseef Ahmed. It was the kind of disciplined defensive innings that Geoff Boycott would have been proud to call his own.

Nobody would associate Boycott with putting the team before himself – he was once dropped by England in 1967 for slow batting even though he had made 246 not out against India – but he inadvertently did so in the Caribbean in 1973–74. By scoring 99 and 112 in a low-scoring final Test in Trinidad, which England won by 26 runs to square the series, Boycott probably kept the captain Mike Denness in a job, perhaps at the expensive of his own captaincy ambitions.

Boycott had a remarkably similar Test average to Adam Gilchrist (47.72 to Gilchrist's 47.60), yet the two were polar opposites. Gilchrist could not have cared less about his average, which made his revolutionary contribution to the game all the more bewildering. One of the many wonders of Gilchrist was that he could, broadly speaking, play both types of attacking innings: if he strolled out at 400-5, he would blast Australia towards a declaration, but arguably he was even scarier at 100-5, because of his capacity to reverse the momentum of a contest inside an hour.

Perhaps the most thrilling example came at Cape Town in 2001–02. In a pivotal Test, with wickets falling like ninepins at the other end, he clinically dissected South Africa's hopes with an innings of 138 from 108 balls. It was a spellbinding example of nerveless momentum-seizing and, in its cruelty, class and sheer bare-faced cheek, it was the purest Gilchrist.

There are, of course, so many other areas in which a player can put the team before himself. Richard Hadlee's fine catch at Brisbane in 1985–86 denied himself a ten-for. Some players have asked to be dropped because of poor form and an inability to help the team, most notably the England captain Mike Denness in 1974–75 and Graham Gooch against the same opposition (and more specifically Terry Alderman) in 1989. Here, again, are the contradictions inherent in our comprehension of the spirit of cricket. Some will doubtless opine that Denness and Gooch demonstrated little more than downright cowardice; others will feel that their selflessness and public admission of weakness was thoroughly admirable.

RICHARD HADLEE
AUSTRALIA V NEW ZEALAND, 1ST TEST, BRISBANE, 8–12 NOVEMBER 1985

Of the myriad disingenuous comments that pollute the world of sport, one of the less believable is the assertion that an individual does not mind failing, provided their team is successful. Goalscorers, new-ball bowlers, rugby wingers . . .

pretty much everything, and everyone, except educated fleas, do it. It is a fact of human nature that self-obsession (or its more socially acceptable sibling, single-mindedness) is invariably a foremost quality, especially among those who attain sporting excellence. All of which makes the behaviour of Richard Hadlee in 1985 so extraordinary.

Hadlee is the greatest cricketer New Zealand has known, a bowler of forensic intelligence and, in sporting terms, a self-made millionaire. He was so superior to his teammates that, in 1986, the England batsman Graham Gooch likened the experience of playing New Zealand to 'facing a World XI at one end and Ilford 2nd XI at the other'. Hadlee's was, to say the least, quite a burden.

The previous winter, New Zealand had visited their bitter rivals Australia. They had never beaten them in a Test series and they had never even won a Test in Australia. Hadlee set about systematically dismantling these unwelcome records. In the first Test at Brisbane, he ripped through the Aussies. Andrew Hilditch fell in the first over, and Hadlee continued to work his way assiduously through the top order. When Craig McDermott was caught by Jeremy Coney, Australia were 175-8 – and Hadlee had taken all eight. With two genuine tailenders to come alongside Geoff Lawson, Hadlee was odds-on to take all ten wickets. It was a feat that, at that stage, had only been achieved once, and has only been repeated once since. Both times it was done by spinners, who had an obvious advantage given their ability to bowl long spells: England's Jim Laker in 1956 and Anil Kumble in 1998–99.

Then it happened. Lawson swiped the debutant spinner

Vaughan Brown over midwicket, and was superbly caught by the man running back. That man was Hadlee, who claimed what was an entirely droppable catch with the business-like economy of a traffic warden fining a crying mother. To Hadlee, circumstances were irrelevant, and there was a job to be done. To ram home what might have been, Hadlee took his ninth wicket a few minutes later.

The spirit of cricket inevitably concentrates on respecting opponents, such is the theoretical capacity for an awkward relationship, but Hadlee showed it is equally important to respect your teammates. It is easy to conclude that of course Hadlee should have caught Lawson, but that is an unfairly simplistic viewpoint. Even with time to make a decision, the majority would be inclined to look after number one, not numbers 1–11; in the heat of battle, with barely a couple of seconds to make a decision, that is inevitably accentuated further.

For that reason, the legendary cricket writer Frank Keating hailed this as this 'the catch of the century'. Hadlee not only processed the needs of the team but also the needs of Vaughan Brown: Lawson was his first and, as it turned out, only Test wicket.

New Zealand went on to win the Test, their first in Australia, with Hadlee taking six more wickets in the second innings (and even helping himself to a half century batting at number 8). And after Australia squared the series in Sydney, Hadlee took another eleven at Perth to give New Zealand the match and the series. It was one of the definitive performances in cricket history. Had Hadlee beaten Australia and taken all ten wickets in an innings, it would have redefined the idea of having your cake and eating it.

But Hadlee did something even better. He had his cake and then decided to share it. 'Afterwards, a number of people said to me, "Why didn't you drop it?"' he later recalled. 'I told them, "The game of cricket's not like that."'

Australia (179 & 333) lost to New Zealand (553-7 dec) by an innings and 41 runs

Poor form is not the sole reason for a player dropping himself: in 1969, on the morning of the Bombay Test against Australia, the Indian swing bowler Subrata Guha agreed to stand down as a response to the fury over the exclusion of Srinivas Venkataraghavan. And in 2004, Nasser Hussain's decision to retire just three days after a matchwinning century against New Zealand at Lord's was partly motivated by a desire to help the selectors avoid a difficult selection decision: with the captain Michael Vaughan injured, his replacement Andrew Strauss had scored 112 and 83 during a glorious debut. With Vaughan fit again, somebody had to go. Hussain did the honourable thing and allowed England to embrace the future, just as he had when he quit unexpectedly as Test captain ten months earlier.

Equally, a player might simply demand a reduced role for the good of the team. On the Ashes tour of 1911–12, the England captain J. W. H. T. Douglas had opened the bowling ahead of the great S. F. Barnes in the first Test – also his debut – but his side were thrashed and, after some extremely bad press and criticism from within his squad, Douglas put the team before his own pride and gave the new ball to Barnes for the second Test at Melbourne.

Barnes took four wickets in the first 35 minutes of the game and England went on to win the series 4–1.

The captain is inevitably in the best position to make decisions that obviously put the team's needs over his own. Mark Taylor received an ovation from his players when he announced that he was to declare when he was 334 not out, 41 shy of the world record and one shy of breaking Don Bradman's record for the highest Test score by an Australian.

MARK TAYLOR
PAKISTAN V AUSTRALIA, 2ND TEST, PESHAWAR, 15–19 OCTOBER 1998

Draws don't come much more honourable than this. It's quite an achievement to score 334 in a Test match and be remembered for the one run you did not score. That was the case with the Australian captain Mark Taylor in Peshawar. Taylor had a fractured night's sleep in the early hours of 17 October 1998. He was obsessed with a milestone which, if achieved, would be the crowning glory of his splendid career. But it was not the one that most would have expected. Taylor was 334 not out, equal with Sir Donald Bradman's record for the highest Test score by an Australian. He was 41 away from Brian Lara's record for the highest Test score of all. Yet the only thing that occupied his mind was whether batting on would increase Australia's chances of victory and clinch their first series victory in Pakistan for 39 years.

In the end Taylor, a man of rare dignity and decency, declared. 'It was typical of his approach to the game that he should be aware of the record without being obsessed by it,' said *Wisden*. 'I did consider batting on, only as a psychological thing with their [Pakistan's] two openers,' Taylor said. 'I knew how good the pitch was and I was just thinking to bat on for 15 minutes just so their openers wouldn't know when they were going to bat. I thought about that option but that's when I thought about the score. I thought if I do bat on for 15 minutes people will only assume I batted on to get 335 and I didn't want people to think that, because that was not the case at all. So, we'd made 599 and I thought "That's plenty of runs to win a Test match, let's go have a bowl."'

As it transpired, he could have batted on to 500 if he wanted: Pakistan easily saved the game on a pitch that was, said *Wisden*, 'made to last a fortnight'. But a week later, a draw in the final Test gave his side that overdue victory in Pakistan. For the consummate team man, that was all that really counted.

Australia (599-4 dec & 289-5) drew with Pakistan (580-9 dec)

Jack Bond, the grizzled, gnarled captain who, in his late thirties, led an effervescent young Lancashire side to five one-day titles between 1969 and 1972, marked their card that the team was all that mattered with a famous declaration at Northampton in 1968, his first year at the helm. Bond, who had not made a first-class century for three years, was 93 not out when he declared. With half an hour left on the second day, he wanted a wicket before the close. He got three, Lancashire won at a canter and the point had been made. 'It made the lads think, nobody can set their own stall out for 100,' said Bond. 'It's the game that matters.'

The spirit of cricket has often had a different meaning: a pre-lunch livener among the members, perhaps. Sometimes it has been in evidence among the players. Garry Sobers says he made one Test century under the influence, having continued drinking to ward off a hangover. In fact, Sobers's exploits were the subject of an entire chapter ('Drunk and Sobers in Nottingham') in the autobiography of the Scottish football legend Jim Baxter.

Harold Larwood loved a discreet pint *on* the field. 'Always had a pint when I was bowling,' he said. 'We used to sneak it in with the soft drinks. A pint for me and one for Bill Voce. You must put back what you sweat out.' When England's left-arm spinner Bobby Peel took six quick wickets to pull off an unexpected victory at Sydney in 1894–95, the first in Tests by a side that had followed on, it was only after he had been held under a cold shower to wash away the effects of industrial quantities of liquor the night before.

Yet the area in which alcohol and cricket have mixed most has been in the post-match beer, a tradition so powerful that it was the subject of a feature in the 2006 *Wisden*. After a hard day in the field, bowlers in particular would be desperate for one for the road they'd just been flogging their guts out on.

The tradition has diminished somewhat in modern times, an inevitable consequence of the increased focus on fitness. Yet in the past it served a vital function: not only did it help to demystify opponents and build friendships, it also, as Sir Ian Botham says, allowed 'the game to cleanse itself'. And if someone eschewed the post-match beer, it was as shocking as a player refusing a handshake. Graham Yallop recalls Mike Brearley saying 'The boys don't want to have a drink with you' during the 1978–79 Ashes, while Allan Border's infamous no-more-Mr-Nice-Guy policy in England in 1989 meant snubbing old friends like Graham Gooch and David Gower, not just after play but before and during it as well. 'Until they'd won the series,' says Gower, 'the only words he said to me were "tails" and occasionally "we'll bat".'

SIR IAN BOTHAM

In my career, the spirit of cricket was about playing tough on the field, not giving an inch, and then having a chat and a beer with the opposition at the end of the day. I just think it was a great way to play the game. You might be in Australia, bowling all day in red-hot conditions. You'd go in, take your boots and wet socks off, and a few minutes later the Aussie boys would arrive with a couple of cold beers. Or if they'd been in the field we'd go in with a few beers. The great thing is the game cleansed itself: if there was a problem, or something that needed sorting, you usually did so there and then. There was no such thing as match referees; there was no need for them.

You might have had D. K. Lillee having a chat with Geoffrey

Boycott, or taking the mick out of him, and as a young bloke you would learn a lot from listening to that – not just about cricket, but about life. People form friendships over a beer; it's an old-fashioned thing called communication. None of this Twitter rubbish. That culture was still going towards the end of my career – I made sure it was – but now it's all professional. You've got to have six gallons of Gatorade and an ice bath, all that bullshit. The sad thing is that, because of that, a lot of the guys don't get to know each other. I made friends in my playing days who will be friends for life.

Sir Ian Botham, England 1977–1992

DAVID GOWER

I've gone for what I call the old Australian way of playing the game, which was that you would have six hours of animated competition on the field and then you would have the chance to sit down and drink with your enemy. I thought that was ideal. You would play the game hard – the original Australian sledging was not a thing of poetic beauty, believe me – but, if you could stomach it, you got to understand the man who might have been trying to knock your head off all day.

I remember batting against Dennis Lillee in Perth, with me as a relative newcomer and him as a superstar of the game. There was all sorts of interaction – looks, raised eyebrows, smiles, plenty of words exchanged – but we managed to build up a degree of mutual respect during it all. That was the Australian way. Then at the end of the day you'd walk off together saying either 'well played' or 'you lucky bastard' and then you'd have a drink.

By doing that you got to know people like Ian Chappell, Greg Chappell, Jeff Thomson, Dennis, Allan Border, and formed really good friendships. When we go back to Perth now there's every chance we'll end up in Dennis Lillee's dining room with a few bottles from his wine collection.

David Gower, England 1978–1992

If there is clear nobility in the idea of the post-match beer, some will also find charm in the laddish pursuits away from the game. To some, David Boon is not so much the stubby run-machine as the man who apparently quaffed 52 stubbies on the flight over for the Ashes tour, beating Rod Marsh's transatlantic record. Terry Alderman's description of Boon at a function the night they arrived – 'he wasn't too crash hot' – hints at a thousand farces, and even though questioning about the subject irks Boon, it will forever be associated with him.

Farce was certainly evident later on the tour: the day after regaining the Ashes at Old Trafford, Australia had to play a tour game at Nottingham. When the stand-in captain Geoff Marsh won the toss on a vicious greentop, his opposite number Tim Robinson could not understand why he had batted first. 'Mate, the boys are still pissed,' Marsh explained, and Merv Hughes recalls a line of bodies strewn across the dressing room, with the next man in being woken up at the fall of each wicket. 'I would suggest,' he said with a soupçon of understatement, 'that was a pretty ugly day.'

The intestinal fortitude of Ian Botham permitted the occasional mid-match bender. After the third day of the Jubilee Test against India in 1979–80, which Botham dominated to a staggering degree with a century and 13 wickets, he went for some zesty evening's entertainment with his teammate Derek Underwood and the journalist Chris Lander. A hideously hungover Lander woke the following day just in time to flick on his TV and see a fiddle-fit Botham celebrating a wicket in the day's first over.

Botham would put his alcohol tolerance to good use for his county. 'Being "Beefed" was a term familiar to most sides heading down to Taunton in the 1980s, as Botham would try to neutralise as many of the visiting team as possible with a whirlwind pub-crawl that would culminate with a lock-in at the infamous Four Alls,' wrote the former Essex and England seamer Derek Pringle, now the cricket correspondent of the *Daily Telegraph*. 'When Surrey visited, he allegedly did such a good job on their fearsome fast bowler Sylvester Clarke that Clarke spent three days sleeping off the hangover on the physio's bench as Somerset took the points.'

In recent years, many a player has winced while recalling the time he was 'Freddied' by Andrew Flintoff. As England searched for the new Ian Botham for a decade and more, it was not just runs and wickets that they sought. Flintoff, memorably, even Freddied himself in the 24 hours following the final Ashes Test of 2005. Social activity is frequently indicative of a healthy team spirit, the existence of which breathes the spirit of cricket. Even those who subscribe to the view of the Scottish footballer Steve Archibald that team spirit is 'an illusion glimpsed in the aftermath of victory' would surely acknowledge that the camaraderie of modern Australian sides, most evident in their fetishisation of the Baggy Green and lusty renditions of 'Under the Southern Cross' when they win a Test, has been a factor in their hegemony. The most improbable triumphs of Duncan Fletcher's reign came on the subcontinent, first in Pakistan and Sri Lanka in 2000–01 and then in India in 2005–06; both were characterised by the kind of unity that cannot be faked. In Sri Lanka they came from behind to win 2–1 despite losing every toss and, in the words of their captain Nasser Hussain, having 'no idea how we were going to even bat a single day'; in Mumbai in 2005–06, a young, makeshift side seemed set to lose the series when India went into lunch on the final day three wickets down. Matthew Hoggard roused spirits with a jaunty blast of Johnny Cash's 'Ring of Fire', a song imbued with hidden, juvenile meaning given the reputation of the local cuisine, and a newly refreshed England hoovered up seven wickets inside 16 delirious overs to win the match and square the series. It was one of the great feelgood triumphs. Another occurred at Sion Mills in 1969, when Ireland, amazingly, skittled the West Indies for 25.

IRELAND V WEST INDIES
TOUR MATCH, SION MILLS, 2 JULY 1969

How can this be comprehended? Ireland did not just beat the West Indies; they bowled them out for 25. And while it was not West Indies' strongest side, more than half had played in the second Test against England at Lord's which finished the previous day. It included Clive Lloyd, Basil Butcher and a 43-year-old Clyde Walcott, now the team manager. There was talk afterwards that David had not so much slayed Goliath as got him blind drunk the night before, although such stories have generally been denied. 'They were very late getting in on the plane and they had a long drive from the airport,' said Douglas Goodwin, the Ireland captain who returned the absurd figures of 12.3-8-6-5. 'We might have had a few, but I don't think they had time to have a drink.'

On a pitch offering appreciable lateral movement, West Indies continued to throw the bat with manic abandon in a desire to entertain. Even though their innings lasted 25.3 overs, all the wickets fell to lusty heaves. They were actually 12-9 until Grayson Shillingford and Philbert Blair more than doubled their score. Ireland passed the score for the loss of one wicket, which explains the slightly unusual scorecard and the apparently contradictory fact that Ireland scored 125-8 and won by nine wickets: the game was a one-day, one-innings contest, but the rules of such matches dictated that, if the side batting second passed their target, the match would continue in case a result could be achieved in a two innings match.

The *Guardian*'s kooky opening paragraph captured the air of disbelief. 'The West Indies were beaten by nine wickets yesterday. Mmm, surprising. It was a one-day match. Well, well. They were all out for 25 runs. Remarkable. Yes, Ireland certainly surprised them. WHO? Ireland – impossible.'

West Indies (25 & 78-4) lost to Ireland (125-8 dec) by 9 wickets

As seductive and lyrical as Archibald's phrase is, eventual victory is not necessary for team spirit to shine through. Warwickshire's extraordinary run of success between 1993 and 1995, when they won six major trophies and, in 1994, were arguably the toss of a coin away from a quadruple, was presaged in a county championship defeat at Hove in 1992. Sussex won by two wickets with one ball to spare, but the way in which Warwickshire overcame a grotesque injury list showed their strength. Their four main seam bowlers, Allan Donald, Gladstone Small, Paul Booth and Dermot Reeve, were all unable to bowl; Keith Piper was unable to keep wicket due to damaged fingers, but still had to field; so did Roger Twose, even though he had required stitches in the face early in the match after being pinned by a Franklyn Stephenson bouncer.

Team spirit can often by engendered by smart captaincy, such as Shane Warne's simple idea to give each of his Rajasthan Royals a playful nickname, which helped to unite a squad drawn from different cultures around the world. Though they were the cheapest franchise in the inaugural Indian Premier League in 2008, they won the competition.

A year earlier, some of Warne's squad had taken part in India's victory at the World Twenty20, a blissful triumph for a young squad without pillars such as Rahul Dravid, Sachin Tendulkar, Sourav Ganguly and Anil Kumble and with no players in their thirties. The optimism and fearlessness of youth effortlessly evokes the spirit of cricket, a fact also evident during the Combined Universities' charming run to the brink of the Benson & Hedges Cup semi-final in 1989.

COMBINED UNIVERSITIES
BENSON & HEDGES CUP, 1989

For those who regard the spirit of cricket to be as much about joy, hope and romance as sportsmanship, there will be few tales to rival that of the Combined Universities in 1989, when they became the first non-first-class side to reach the quarter-finals of the Benson & Hedges Trophy. They should have gone even further, but heartbreakingly blew a winning position against Somerset in the quarter-finals.

Their team included future England captains in Mike Atherton and Nasser Hussain, as well as Steve James, the Glamorgan opener who played two Tests. They qualified from the five-team group stage by beating Surrey and then hammering the county champions

Worcestershire, for whom Ian Botham was one of seven past, present and future Test players in the side, by five wickets. The *Guardian* described it as 'the finest-ever limited-overs performance'. In the same week Worcestershire would beat Australia inside two days in a first-class match; Australia would go on to regain the Ashes 4–0.

This was stirring stuff. It certainly stirred Botham, who had been dismissed for 0 and who stormed out of the shared shower-room outlining his thoughts on students. Later that night, when the team were refused entry to a nightclub, Adrian Dale announced that that afternoon he had got Ian Botham out for a duck. To the unimpressed bouncers, it was another likely story.

The campaign was full of such fond memories. Nasser Hussain, one of five Durham students in the side, fondly recalls them hiring a minibus to get to games and stopping off for fish and chips in Wetherby on the way home. James Boiling, the off-spinner who played for Surrey and England A, recalls being among two dozen people huddled round a TV in his hall of residence to watch *Grandstand* – except this time Boiling was on it, in a pre-recorded interview with the broadcaster Ralph Dellor. Not that the majority could cash in on their newfound celebrity: in the fortnight between the group stages and the quarter-final they were sitting their final exams. Steve James even missed the quarter-final because Cambridge would not release him.

Durham were more understanding: Hussain and Martin Speight were allowed to take theirs a day early and had a chaperone for the next 24 hours. The home side batted first but, despite being 208 for two at one point, they were never really in control on a flat track. The Universities' tactic of hurtling through their overs – they managed a staggering 46 in the two-and-a-quarter-hour session before lunch on a couple of occasions – was a magic trick that made opponents think they had more time left than was actually the case. 'We played the sort of cricket that helped Gloucestershire win a load of one-day trophies in the nineties,' says Hussain. 'Choking and containing teams, with the keeper standing up. In an age of Malcolm Marshall, Courtney Walsh and Sylvester Clarke, teams weren't really used to it.'

That relentless over rate was made possible by a number of spinners with barely a run-up, including a richly promising young legspinner by the name of Atherton, who took four for 42 against Somerset. An eventual target of 253 in 55 overs was entirely gettable. Even more so when, after a slow start, Hussain came out and started creaming off-drives in a manner that would become familiar. His eventual metamorphosis into a crotchety grinder has partially obscured what a brilliant talent he possessed. 'He was the best of his age group in the country,' says Speight. 'You would not believe how good he was.'

Hussain made a simply glorious century, and added 114 in 17 overs for the fourth wicket with Jon Longley. That left the Universities on 223 for three, needing 30 off 36 balls. A cakewalk, ordinarily, but then the gravity of their imminent achievement began to impact: Longley slapped his bête noire Adrian Jones to point, and Hussain was crucially deprived of the strike as the lower order struggled to deal with the liquorice-allsorts spin of Peter Roebuck, a canny old pro.

'To be bowled out by one of the greats is fair enough, but to lose to Peter Roebuck's legspin still haunts me,' says Hussain. 'We were just a bit bamboozled. Up to a certain point we didn't realise what we were achieving, and then when we did the pressure took hold.'

The final over, from Roebuck, came with nine needed, but Chris Tolley was stumped and then, with eight needed from four balls, Hussain drove to deep mid-off. 'I can't remember how I got out,' laughs Hussain. 'Caught deep mid-off? With the power of my shots I bet it was mid-off diving forward!' Boiling was left with the not-inconsiderable task of hitting his first ball, the last of the match, for six to make history. He could only manage two and the Universities were out. Atherton said that 'it was as disappointed a dressing room as I've ever been in. We bottled it basically.'

And that was that. The players had to head off that evening because of exams and were never together as a group again, their lives set on different roads. The romance of their tale seems impossible in the modern age — at the time, Twenty20 was the rancid fruity booze you bought if there was no Lambrini left at the Spar. 'There was an amateur spirit which was so refreshing,' said Boiling, 'and the further removed I am from it the stronger that feels.'

Brotherhoods were evident through that university side, as they have been throughout cricket history. Opening partnerships, new-ball pairs, spin twins, wicketkeeper and bowler. Not that it's exclusive to duos. The West Indies' quartet of pacemen was a constant for 15 years and, while their modus operandi was not to all tastes, the sense of unity was palpable. There is a brilliant photo of the Windies' first great pace attack, with Michael Holding, Andy Roberts, Joel Garner and Colin Croft (Malcolm Marshall came later) stood in line on a parched outfield at the Kensington Oval in Bridgetown.

The flipside was India's holy trinity of spinners: the beguiling left-armer Bishen Bedi, the offspinner Erapalli Prasanna and the legspinner Bhagwat Chandrasekhar. Occasionally Srinivas Venkataraghavan turned them into a quartet. Further back there was the South African quartet of googly bowlers – Aubrey Faulkner, Reggie Schwarz, Ernie Vogler and Gordon White – who bewildered the entire England squad except Jack Hobbs in 1909–10.

Yet in a sense there is greater charm in the improbable tryst, like George Hirst and Wilfred Rhodes getting 'em in singles at The Oval in 1902, apocryphal though the story might be. Or a number 11 desperately trying to see a senior batsman to a century, or, better still, to win or save a match. Occasionally they have managed both: in a rain-affected match against the West Indies at The Oval in 1980, England were 92-9, a lead of 197, when Bob Willis arrived to join Peter Willey with nearly two sessions to play. As well as saving the game in an unbroken last-wicket partnership of 117, Willis survived long enough to see Willey – who had not reached 20 when the pair came together – to a maiden Test century and the Man of the Match award. Six hours earlier he had seemed likely to be dropped.

GAVIN LARSEN/ROD LATHAM/
CHRIS HARRIS
1992 WORLD CUP

Cricket has produced myriad unlikely brotherhoods, but perhaps have none has been quite as charmingly improbable as the tale of Gavin Larsen, Chris Harris and Rod Latham, the triumvirate of slow medium-pacers who starred as New Zealand moved unstoppably through the extended league stage at the 1992 World Cup.

With their playful nicknames of Dibbly, Dobbly and Wobbly, they sounded like cricket's answer to the Teletubbies. They certainly spoke a language batsmen couldn't understand: on pitches seemingly made of porridge, they slowly, surely absorbed any attacking intent the batting side had to offer during the middle overs.

At times they were unhittable, especially Larsen, an immaculate line-and-length merchant who was parsimony incarnate and went for just 3.44 runs per over throughout the tournament. He took 3 – 30 in the opening victory over Australia, and was so consistent that he produced identical figures of 10-1-29-0 in consecutive games.

Harris, with his slow-slow-trick variations, was more of an attacking threat and took 13 wickets, the joint third-highest in the tournament. Latham, in the side mainly as an opener, was the ugly sister of the three: he took only one wicket in the tournament and went for 5.91 per over. But without him, the legend of the three tortoises of the apocalypse would not be complete.

The Man of the Match award is very occasionally shared by two members of the same side, a sure sign of a shared journey to remember. That was the case at Johannesburg in 1995, when Mike Atherton (185 not out from 492 balls) and Jack Russell (29 not out from 235 balls) famously repelled South Africa. An already unforgettable alliance was infused with further charm but the opposite nature of the two characters: Atherton the strong, silent type, Russell the eccentric chatterbox.

Even more memorable, perhaps, are those times when players from opposing sides show that they are *simpatico* – particularly when they have previously engaged in some form of conflict. When Manny Martindale knocked Bob Wyatt unconscious, breaking his jaw in four places, with a short one at Jamaica in 1934–35, Wyatt wrote to Martindale from hospital to absolve him of any blame. When Wyatt later travelled from the hospital to the airport, Martindale was there to see him off.

The Bodyline series was over 15 years old when Jack Fingleton, one of Australia's openers in that series, walked into Harold Larwood's sweetshop in Blackpool and set in motion a process that would end with Larwood settling happily in Australia.

ANDY BULL

If you wanted to capture the spirit of cricket in a sentence you would be hard pushed to improve on this: 'Cricket civilises people and creates good gentlemen.' Robert Mugabe said that in 1984. If you needed a steer as to just how misplaced the misty-eyed sentiment of the spirit of cricket has become, that seems a good start.

Cricket has no claim on the moral high ground among sports, and never has done. It has always had its fair share of bounders, cheats and scoundrels. It first thrived, after all, as a vehicle for mass gambling and gaming in the 17th century. The phoney baloney morality of 'it's just not cricket' came later, with the Victorian gentry.

If I had to pick one single example of a cricketing act that transcended simple good sportsmanship I would go back to a morning in 1957, when a letter from South Africa landed on John Arlott's doormat. Arlott was a poet, police officer and cricket commentator. The letter, written in green ink, came from a complete stranger on the on the other side of the world.

It had been written by Basil D'Oliveira, 26. He was, as we now know, a prodigiously talented player from Cape Town who was prevented from proving himself in first-class cricket by racial segregation. He had never spoken to Arlott, but he was writing in the hope that he could help him find a club to play for in the UK.

After much work, Arlott helped secure D'Oliveira a place with Middleton in the Lancashire League. Given that start, D'Oliveira went on to qualify for England, and played in 44 Tests.

The familiarity of the story makes it all seem such a natural course of events. But I wonder how many people would, receiving that letter, have simply ignored it, or offered a simple 'sorry, I can't help but good luck' in reply. It was only through Arlott's kindness and generosity of spirit that D'Oliveira was able to come to England. His letter back to South Africa set in course a train of events that would eventually lead to the sport taking a genuinely noble moral stance, the decision in 1970 to refuse to play with a country in which apartheid existed.

Andy Bull is a cricket writer for the Guardian

Such displays of generosity need not involve those who have been in direct competition. John Arlott was instrumental in bringing Basil D'Oliveira over from South Africa, while Viv Richards's story would have followed a different path were it not for the generosity of Colin Cowdrey and Len Creed, a Bath bookmaker and vice-chairman of Somerset. Cowdrey, having played against the young Richards in Antigua, described him as 'promising' in *The Cricketer* in 1973. It triggered something in Creed, who flew to Antigua on a whim and brought Richards back with him. After a year playing league cricket for Lansdown in Bath, Richards was ready to manhandle county attacks. As he took the Match Award for a cool unbeaten 81 on his Somerset debut, in a Benson & Hedges Cup match away to Glamorgan, he looked up to see Creed in tears.

JACK FINGLETON AND HAROLD LARWOOD
BLACKPOOL, 1948

To most Australians, Harold Larwood might have been an ogre during the Bodyline series of 1932–33: inscrutable and unstoppable as he terrorised Australia's batsmen with what seemed like a frightening lack of emotion. Yet the Australian opener Jack Fingleton, one of the more englightened men to ever play the game, saw the humanity within. Despite taking some awful blows during the series, he became fascinated with Larwood, a fascination that was still in evidence 15 years later when he came to England to cover the Invincibles tour as a journalist.

The two had always shared a mutual respect: Fingleton called Larwood 'the master'; in return, Larwood said that Fingleton was the bravest batsman he had ever bowled to. Fingleton was shocked and saddened to hear that Larwood – who had been unforgiveably scapegoated and ostracised by the MCC in the aftermath of Bodyline, never playing another Test even though he was just 28 when the series ended – was down on his luck, running a sweetshop in Blackpool, as bruised by life's vicissitudes as the Australian batsmen had been by his application of leg-theory. George Duckworth, the former England wicketkeeper who was also working as a journalist, told Fingleton that Larwood was 'a lonely, desolate chap and would love to see you'.

Duncan Hamilton, Larwood's biographer, wrote that 'Like Robinson Crusoe after the storm, there was an element of the shipwrecked mariner about Larwood in Blackpool. He was wave-tossed and had salvaged what he could from the buffeting of Bodyline.' Fingleton made it his business to visit the shop as soon as possible with Duckworth and, after an initial awkwardness, the three loosened up over a few ales.

They ended up back at the sweetshop, a little the worse for wear, and Fingleton suggested a simple solution to Larwood's unhappiness: emigration to Australia. The idea proved irresistible to Larwood, who recalled the startlingly generous reception he received at Sydney when he was made 98 as a nightwatchman in the final Bodyline Test. Fingleton greased the appropriate wheels and even arranged for the prime minster, Ben Chifley, to greet Larwood when he eventually arrived in Sydney. He would live, if not happy ever after, then content, free of the burning frustration that was ruining his life in England.

Viv Richards dealt in deed rather than word at the crease, and his laconic nature magnified his already formidable presence. As Scyld Berry says, Richards 'walked the walk before anyone thought of the phrase'. Yet occasionally he talked the talk too. In the mid-eighties Glamorgan's young Welsh paceman Greg

Thomas slipped one past Richards's outside edge in a county match and followed up by saying: 'It's red, it's round and it weighs about five ounces.' Richards dumped the next ball out of the ground before announcing imperiously: 'You know what it looks like, go and fetch it.'

Sledging might not be the first thing that springs to mind when you think about the spirit of cricket, but a good one-liner reinforces cricket's perception as a game of wit and whimsy. Frank Tyson, England's terrifyingly fast new-ball bowler in the fifties, would frequently quote Shakespeare and Wordsworth to batsmen. When Shaun Pollock, captain of the hosts South Africa, came out to bat at Durban in 2003, with his side on the brink of going out of their own World Cup at the first stage, the Sri Lankan wicketkeeper-batsman (and avid sledger) Kumar Sangakkara began musing on the state of the game to his teammates: 'Lot of pressure for the skipper, yeah? Gonna let his whole country down if he fails. Lots of expectations, fellas. Ah, man, the weight of all those expectations . . . forty-two million supporters depending on Shaun.' Later that year, when an under-pressure Nasser Hussain came out to bat in a Test match at Kandy, Sangakkara greeted him with a burst of the Everly Brothers song 'Bye Bye Love': 'Bye bye love, bye bye happiness, hello loneliness, I feel I'm going to cry.'

It's a measure of Andrew Flintoff's joie de vivre that his 'Mind the windows' comment to the West Indian tailender Tino Best would make many lists of the greatest Flintoff moments. And even Merv Hughes, a man who usually had a strike rate of one cuss every second word, came up with a few memorable witticisms. When Pakistan's Javed Miandad described him as a 'fat bus conductor', Hughes celebrated the dismissal of Miandad soon after with a joyous shot of 'Tickets please!'

In 1898, Charles Kortright had dismissed W. G. Grace on a number of occasions, only for the umpires to be blinded by Grace's personality and repeatedly give him not out. Kortright eventually knocked two stumps out of the ground and, as WG trudged off reluctantly, applied a superb *coup de grâce*: 'Surely you're not going, Doc? There's still one stump standing.' Then there is Paul Nixon, the England wicketkeeper who some described as a specialist sledger when he came into the side ahead of the 2007 World Cup. He came, he swore, he conquered. In the event, Nixon more than justified his place, with excellent keeping and innovative, fearless batting, but he will be best remembered for his sledging, the consequences of which were often comedic. When Nixon came up against his old Kent teammate, Australia's Andrew Symonds, he informed Symonds that he was going to catch him and then send him the scorecard every day for a year. Symonds's response was to belabour the ball with such intensity that he ruptured a bicep muscle and almost missed the upcoming World Cup.

ALAN DAVIES

I played in Arthur Smith's team, which is called the Dusty Fleming's International Hairstylists XI, named after a series of ridiculous TV commercials in the nineties. It was made up of various actors, comedians, writers and all kinds of reprobates. Arthur encouraged sledging, and the funnier the better. Good sledging was basically the reason everyone was on the pitch. We would play against a team put together by Chris England, who was Arthur's writing partner, and they took it much more seriously: they would practise a lot and had all the kit, whereas Arthur was much more about going to the pub before and after. We also had the annual awards dinner-dance, where there were awards for things like 'Best catch taken while smoking'. That's only ever happened once, but the award still exists.

Chris England was at university with Hugh Grant, and he turned up once when I wasn't there. Apparently Liz Hurley, who was his girlfriend at the time, came along and was wearing hotpants, so from that day Arthur would urge Chris to select Hugh. He'd just been out in America, and apparently Madonna had made some comments about how she wanted to have dinner and a bit else with him. He hadn't gone along to meet her, and it had been a big thing in the papers. So Matthew Hardy, who was quite a broad, ocker Aussie, shouted from the boundary: 'Get this c*** out, he turned down Madonna!' It made everyone fall about. Hugh Grant just smiled broadly and took his guard...

ANDREW FLINTOFF
ENGLAND V WEST INDIES, 1ST TEST, LORD'S, 22–26 JULY 2004

The glorious mid-noughties era of English cricket ended sadly, with injuries, fall-outs and increasing incompetence, but for a wonderful two-year period they were having some serious fun. They were winning games – 16 out of 23 in 2004–05, with only two losses – and were basically a group of mates having a great time. Nothing encapsulated that better than Freddie Flintoff's mischievous sledging of the West Indian tailender Tino Best at Lord's in 2004.

With England cruising to victory on the final day, Flintoff decided to settle a score with Best. In Trinidad during the reverse series three months earlier, Best had riled Flintoff by going through his delivery motion even though he did not have the ball in his hand, leaving Flintoff to think he had lost sight of a beamer and was about to be hit on the head. 'I'm the first one to enjoy a laugh and a joke on the field and there are some things you can do,' said Flintoff, 'but that was just not one of them.'

His chance for payback came with the impetuous Best denying his basic instincts by diligently blocking Ashley Giles. 'Mind the windows, Tino!' chirped Flintoff from slip. Inevitably, Best tried to put Giles through one of those windows, missed completely and was stumped by yards. Flintoff celebrated with the mischievous grin of a child who has just seen a teacher sit on his whoopee cushion. 'Now that *was* a good laugh,' said Flintoff. Others highlighted the important symbolism of an England player making a West Indian look silly, a reversal of decades of humiliation, but it's highly unlikely that was in Flintoff's mind. He was just having fun. In those days, when the results of the team kept the fun police quiet, Freddie was both Messiah and lovably naughty boy.

England (568 & 325-5 dec) beat West Indies (416 & 267) by 210 runs

Sledging at its best is a mark of respect for rather than hostility towards opponents, and those who show consideration for friend and foe alike are usually imbued with a sense of the spirit of cricket. For decades, a culture of 'one off the mark' – giving a new batsman a single if he was, say, on his debut or on a pair – prevailed. One of the more famous examples involved the great West Indian batsman George Headley on his return to Test cricket after a six-year absence against England in Kingston in 1953–54, when Len Hutton deliberately set the field back for the bowler Tony Lock. Astonishingly, when Jim Laker took 8-2 for England against The Rest in a Test trial at Bradford in 1950, one of the runs he conceded was a gentle one off the mark for his mate Eric Bedser. 'I was obliged to honour an agreement made earlier on the train,' said Laker.

The reverse runs equally true, with many batsmen giving their wicket away out of respect for the opposition. The marvellous Australian Keith Miller, who had no truck with phoney achievement, famously offered no shot to his first ball against Essex in 1948; in 1954–55, Miller's new-ball partner Ray Lindwall was given a Test wicket by England's Trevor Bailey, who allowed himself to be bowled, thinking it would be Lindwall's last Test wicket. As it

THE SPIRIT OF CRICKET

transpired, he was still around four years later and bowled Bailey in more authentic fashion. And then there was Jack Hobbs, who had none of the murderous ambition of other great runscorers and who usually felt his job was done when he reached a century, at which point he would frequently and unobtrusively grant his wicket to the bowler he felt most deserving.

The England all-rounder Trevor Bailey was himself the beneficiary of an opponent's generosity. Speaking in his guise as the biographer of the great Barbadian Garry Sobers, he recalls Sobers gifting his wicket in a benefit match in the sixties. 'It is easy to give one's wicket away,' wrote Bailey, 'but it takes an artist to do this as well as Garry did to me. It was the way he did it which typified both the man and his craft. He played deliberately and fractionally down the wrong line. He made it look a very good delivery. I knew instinctively what Garry had done. But no spectator realised it was an act of charity; only Garry and myself.'

KEITH MILLER
ESSEX V THE AUSTRALIANS, TOUR MATCH,
SOUTHEND-ON-SEA, 15–17 MAY 1948

On 15 May 1948, the Australians scored 721 runs, still a world record for a single day's play, yet the most notable performance came from a man who scored exactly none of them: Keith Miller, who allowed himself to be bowled first ball as a protest against what he perceived as vulgar bullying of an inferior team.

Having spent the Second World War never knowing whether each day would be his last, Miller had more perspective than most. 'Pressure is a Messerschmitt up your arse,' he said to Michael Parkinson. 'Playing cricket is not.' But his experiences did not just grant him immunity to pressure; they also made him aware of the qualitative value of achievement.

One-sided cricket held no interest for such a natural performer, and taking 721 pieces of candy disgusted him; so did seeing honest county cricketers humiliated. When he walked to the crease at 364-2, with his ideological opposite Don Bradman well on the way to a remorseless 187, Miller did not plan on staying long. He did not even bother to take guard, played no shot to an off-cutter from Trevor Bailey (yes, him again), flicked his hair back and walked off saying 'Thank God that's over' to anyone within earshot. 'He'll learn,' muttered an exasperated Bradman. Some reports even suggest Miller had turned on his heels before the ball hit the stumps.

'If ever a single situation could be said to epitomise the man,' wrote Mihir Bose in his biography of Miller, 'then this was it.' For a man who could not have cared less about averages, it is fitting that a duck was one of his signature performances.

Australia (721) beat Essex (83 & 187) by an innings and 451 runs

Other gestures of sportsmanship include allowing last-minute or mid-match team changes. During the 2009 Ashes series, both England and Australia suffered injuries to wicketkeepers on the eve of Test matches. When Brad Haddin broke a finger in practice after the teams had been handed in for the third Test, England allowed Graham Manou to take his place; when Matt Prior injured his back playing football on the morning of the fourth Test, Australia agreed to put the toss back ten minutes to give England more time to ascertain Prior's fitness.

There can be no greater gesture towards an opponent, however, than granting them a deserved victory. These days, all sides are more than happy to embrace a moral defeat, so long as they get an actual draw. That was not always the case. In 1905, the Australian captain Joe Darling made his team bat in dodgy light because his conscience told him that England had been much the better team and deserved to win. Sussex did the same when they came out to play in pouring rain against Warwickshire in 1924.

'The spectators rose to them – all fifty of us,' wrote Rowland Ryder in *Wisden*. "Well played, Mr. Gilligan," called a voice in a rich Birmingham accent. We buttoned up our mackintoshes and went home in the never-ending rain, warmed by the sunshine of Sussex.'

When Nottinghamshire did the opposite in 1935, leaving the field because of rain with Sussex needing two runs to win, it caused an almighty storm. Sussex threatened not to play Nottinghamshire again, while Nottinghamshire set up a committee which concluded it was 'a flagrant offence against the spirit of cricket'.

England certainly felt that winning (or drawing) was not everything when they emerged in the rain to complete a defeat to Barbados on the 1959–60 tour of the Caribbean. With time running out on the final day of the first Victory Test of 1945, Alf

Gover ensured his England team ran to their positions before 7 p.m. so that Australia would receive the extra over they needed to complete a deserved victory. Rod Marsh felt the same when he shook his head sadly as Trevor Chappell bowled his infamous underarm delivery to secure a win over New Zealand in 1979. And when Pakistan tried to slow England's victory march at Karachi in 2000–01, the umpire Steve Bucknor told the captain Moin Khan that they would play until a result was achieved, no matter what. England won in pitch darkness.

THE 2005 ASHES

Wearing sunglasses in dark conditions may be chic in certain circles but when the Australian team did so at The Oval in 2005 their reasons were much more virtuous. On the penultimate day of that series, which was frequently affected by bad light and rain, there was an amusing tug of war: England, who needed only a draw to regain the Ashes for the first time in 16 years, were happy to be off the field, whereas Australia were desperate to be on it.

Yet the enormous stakes did not impinge upon the chivalry that prevailed for all bar a few minutes of the series. First Andrew Flintoff jokily informed the umpire Rudi Koertzen that he couldn't even see the bails; then, after a short break, Australia came back on to the field in gloomy conditions all wearing sunglasses.

The series was defined by goodwill. The famous embrace between Andrew Flintoff and Brett Lee. Shane Warne calling after

Flintoff to applaud him and say 'well played' following Flintoff's brave 73 in the second Test at Edgbaston. The standing ovation for Warne when he took his 600th Test wicket at Old Trafford. The crowd singing 'We wish you were English' to him on the final day of the series. And Australia, to a man, lining up to admit that England had been too good for them.

Only twice did that fall down. First, when England failed to enquire about Ricky Ponting's health when Steve Harmison drew blood at Lord's. Secondly, when Ponting launched a stream of invective at the England coach Duncan Fletcher. Given the unparalleled intensity of the matches, that level of sporting goodwill is a minor miracle.

Respect for opponents and those on the pitch extends beyond those on the pitch. It might manifest itself in a club refusing to employ Kolpak players – those from certain countries, chiefly South Africa, who are permitted to play as non-overseas players as a consequence of the European Court of Justice ruling in favour of Maroš Kolpak, a Slovak handball player, in a case regarding the freedom of movement in 2003 – or in honest pitch preparation. Australia, the home of the quintessential good cricket wicket, had their suspicions after The Oval 2009 and particularly Old Trafford 1956, when Jim Laker took 19 wickets, but generally England have been renowned for not tailoring wickets. Just ask Muttiah Muralitharan, who took 16 and 11 wickets on horrid dustbowls at The Oval in 1998 and Trent Bridge in 2006. England have helped opposing spinners in quirkier ways, too:

when the West Indian left-armer Alf Valentine toured in 1950, he struggled to read the scoreboard in an early tour match. After receiving a pair of NHS glasses, stuck together with sticking plaster, almost every day of the series was Valentines's Day: he took 33 wickets in his debut series.

Valentine's performance, in tandem with Sonny Ramadhin, transcended those bald statistics. Yet if numbers are far from the be-all and end-all of cricket, as we have seen, then the extent to which cricket produces them – unique outside American sports – offers scope for the kind of nerdy fascination that is the preserve of cricket. The advent of Cricinfo's remarkable statsguru facility, created by Travis Basevi, has led to the use of statsguru as a verb; have you statsgurued your favourite player lately? If so, be sure to statsguru responsibly: statistics, like alcohol, should be treated maturely and in moderation. Among the trillions of statistics cricket has produced, Don Bradman's average stands alone, but there are so many others. The Don, of course, does not have the highest Test average. That belongs to the West Indian opener Andy Ganteaume, who made 112 in his only Test innings, against England in 1947–48, and was dropped, some say for slow scoring. At least Ganteaume's claim to fame related to the correct discipline. Geoff Allott, a very decent New Zealand left-armer who was joint top-wicket taker in the 1999 World Cup, is best remembered for making a 77-ball 0 against South Africa a few months earlier.

Absurd statistics are part of cricket's charm, and in almost infinite supply. There is an endearing perversity about a game in which, in real terms, 9 can be higher than 190. Certainly some would argue that Alec Stewart's 9 not out in the abandoned Test at Sabina Park in 1997–98 had more going for it than his 190 on an Edgbaston featherbed against Pakistan in 1992. Then there is Brian Lara. Just as Bradman will forever be associated with 99.94, so Lara's career was studded with very large numbers, probably more than any other: 501, 400, 375, 277, and so on. Yet the best of them all was probably a comparatively humble 153 not out, when West Indies beat Australia by one wicket in one of the great Test matches, in Barbados in 1998–99.

DON BRADMAN'S AVERAGES

It is the equivalent of the two-minute mile. Don Bradman's Test average of 99.94, almost 40 per cent ahead of the next best among those who have played more than a couple of Tests, almost defies comprehension. It was given a chapter of its own in Ed Smith's book *What Sport Tells Us About Life* and is as memorable a number as a son's date of birth is to his mother. If you ever rob a cricket fan and don't know his PIN, try 9994 first. In Australia, ABC radio has the address, GPO Box 9994, while an old office that was shared by Cricinfo and *The Wisden Cricketer* had a passcode of 9994.

Some of the component parts of that average are even more startling. He averaged 201.50 against South Africa and 178.75

against India. In 1932 he averaged 402. At Headingley he averaged 192.60. In the 30 Tests he played that Australia won, he averaged 130.08 and converted an astonishing 86 per cent of his fifties into hundreds: 23 out of 27. For all that, Bradman also knew failure. He could be a slow starter, and over 10 per cent of his Test innings ended at 0 or 1 – including, most famously of all, his last at The Oval in 1948. Needing four to complete a Test average of 100, Bradman was given three cheers by the England team and bowled second ball for nought by Eric Hollies' googly. It was a perverse note on which to end, but also a charming one: not even Bradman, the genius as automaton, could quite write his own script.

The same is true of bowlers. The off-spinner Pat Pocock once took seven wickets in 11 balls for Surrey against Sussex in 1972, yet feels he bowled better when he took 0-152 for England in a Test match in Jamaica. The noble nought-for has a charm all of its own. Andrew Flintoff's breakthrough performance as an England bowler came when he took 0-80 in 34 overs of the hardest yakka against India at Mohali in 2001–02. By the same token, five-fors can have little value whatsoever: it is safe to assume that Glenn McGrath's grandchildren will not be hearing about his 5-115 at Old Trafford in 2005, when he went at nearly six an over and two of his wickets were out caught in the deep.

Others would wish they could pick and choose in such a way. There is huge poignancy in the tales of players who get within a whisker of a Test century, never to make it. Martyn Moxon, the Yorkshire and England opener, was dismissed for 99 against New

Zealand in 1987–88, but early in his innings three swept runs were wrongly given as leg-byes. He would never get so close to a Test century again. The Pakistan batsman Zahid Fazal was forced to retire hurt with cramp on 98 during a Sharjah one-dayer against India in 1991. At the age of 18 he probably thought he would have umpteen opportunities to make a century for his country, but it did not happen and he played his last international at 21.

Statistics can be dangerous when elevated to an inappropriate level of significance, but by the same token it would be remiss to simply accept the notion that there are lies, damned lies and statistics. When the New Zealand fast bowler Shane Bond retired from Test cricket at the end of 2009, nothing emphasised his impact better than a look at New Zealand's performance with and without him since his Test debut. With Bond they had won 10, drawn 6 and lost 2; without him they had won 15, drawn 15 and lost 24.

The quantitative nature of cricket can also highlight purple patches or extreme vagaries of form in a way that other sports might not allow. In the 1989 Ashes, Steve Waugh scored 393 runs before being dismissed; when he was finally bowled by Angus Fraser, it felt like Goliath had been slain. Another Australian champion, Ricky Ponting, had one of the game's more absurd runs of form in Test series against Pakistan and India in 1999–2000, when he followed three consecutive ducks with innings of 197 and 125. In 1982–83, the classy Indian middle-order batsman Mohinder Amarnath ignored the wreckage at the other end to score 598 runs at an average of 66.44 in five Tests in the

Caribbean. All was set fair for the return series. Amarnath made just one run in six innings.

An identical run befell the serene Sri Lankan opener Marvan Atapattu in his first three Tests – to compound the not inconsiderable misery, those innings were spread over four years, and it was almost seven years from his debut when Atapattu finally scored his second Test run. Yet despite having all that time to contemplate potentially the most ignominious Test career of them all, he went on to score 5,502 runs, including six double centuries. Not that his duck-habit fully deserted him: he ended up with 22, a record for a top-order batsman.

To some this will all be an irrelevance, but that is simply another example of the endearing contradictions evident in our understanding of the spirit of cricket. Try telling a statistics-oriented anorak that Atapattu's tale is not part of cricket's charm. Even those who don't care for statistics might be moved by the impossible cuteness of Australia's winning margin over England in the Centenary Test: 45 runs, just as it was in the very first Test match 100 years earlier.

That Australian side was captained by Ian Chappell, an Aussie to the core and a man who galvanised the toughest of units through an overt hostility towards the opposition and, where necessary, an unashamed siege mentality. To some that might contradict the spirit of cricket, yet Chappell is not the only captain to take such a view. Take the Sri Lankan captain Arjuna Ranatunga, who led his side off the field when Muttiah Muralitharan was no-balled for throwing in a one-day match against England by the umpire Ross Emerson.

Ranatunga was given a suspended six-match ban, but remained unrepentant. 'The spirit of cricket invokes not only the wonderful characteristic of sportsmanship but also the virtues of teamwork and loyalty to one's teammates and superiors,' he said. 'Sometimes these qualities can find themselves in competition. My actions following the no-balling of Murali were motivated by my responsibility to demonstrate support for him in that situation.' Proof, if ever it were needed, that the spirit of cricket is never black and white.

RICKY PONTING

I have been so fortunate to be one of just over 400 Australians who have worn the Baggy Green for Australia. Every day I feel very proud to be part of this select group and the Baggy Green is a powerful symbol of the great honour bestowed on me and my fellow Australian Test cricketers. During my time as a member of the Australian team, the symbolism of the Baggy Green has become more meaningful from era to era. Steve Waugh did an incredible job in making it a fundamental part of the Australian team and indeed a tangible representation of the honour of playing cricket for our country. I have strived hard to carry on this tradition in my time as Australian captain; indeed, the condition of my own Baggy Green over the past six months has been the cause of great concern for me. If you compare photos of my Baggy Green from the final day of the Oval Test match in August 2009 to its state at the end of the Sydney

Test against Pakistan in January 2010, you will see a significant deterioration in its appearance and condition. My Baggy Green represents everything that has come down to me in Australian cricket tradition and the role that I play today and into the future of the game in my country. During the Pakistan Test series, many retired Australian stars called on me to start wearing a new Baggy Green, saying that I was being disrespectful of the tradition of Australian cricket by wearing a damaged cap. But my view is that it is my responsibility to carry on the captain's tradition of the Baggy Green, so deeply imbued in me by Steve Waugh (who experienced a similar issue with his Baggy Green late in his career), and the last thing I want to do is to start wearing a new Baggy Green. At the end of the Sydney Test I went to Albion, who make the Baggy Green caps, and asked them to do a full repair before the Hobart Test ten days later. As you may have seen in photos from that Test, they did a fantastic repair job and I am now confident that my Baggy Green will stay with me right through to my retirement from Test cricket – just the way it should be! My Baggy Green represents the spirit of cricket to me. Sure I have many other great life experiences, from my early childhood riding my BMX all over Launceston to watch my local Mowbray side play, to the highs and lows of my time as a batter in the Australian team and then in my role as captain of the Australian team. The dressing-room traditions of the Australian team, the great teammates and opponents on the field and the wonderful moments that I have observed and been part of are also very special to me. But they don't come close to the essence of the Baggy Green, which I treasure as the single most significant symbol of my career and of the real spirit of Australian cricket.

Ricky Ponting, Australia 1995–

CHAPTER FOUR

Life, says the American writer Marvin Cohen, is an elaborate metaphor for cricket. Cricket, says the former Indian seamer Atul Wassan, is a metaphor for life. 'What you can see happening on a cricket field can invariably be related to what is going in the real world,' says Richie Benaud. 'Sometimes joy, sometimes warts and all.' The comparison, admittedly, is not to all tastes. 'If anyone had a fish supper for every time it was mentioned that something was not cricket, or that the noble game was a metaphor for life, they'd be up there with two-ton Tessie O'Shea,' said the *Guardian*'s Mike Selvey in 1999. 'It's the cliché's cliché.'

That is certainly true, but nonetheless it is hard to think of a sport that has looked so proudly and inquisitively beyond its boundaries. As a consequence, cricket has the capacity to be a reference point for all aspects of life, starting with the everyday phrase 'it's not cricket' to signify that which is immoral. It can apply to the most serious of matters, or the most frivolous. When, during the Second World War, Mussolini was defeated in 1943, a

Tory MP said: 'We have got Ponsford out cheaply, but Bradman is still batting.' At the other end of the scale, scarcely anybody would have imagined that Mark Ramprakash, such a tortured presence in his sadly unfulfilled Test career, would display such freedom and joie de vivre on *Strictly Come Dancing*.

It is not remotely trite to say that cricket serves as a civilising force. The great Kumar Ranjitsinhji called it 'one of the greatest contributions which the greatest people have made to the cause of humanity'. In 1948, a list of religious services in the *Guardian* included 'It's not cricket', to be read at the Albert Hall in Manchester by the Reverend Stanley E. Parsons and the Reverend J. Russell Pope.

TONY GREIG

We tend to think of the spirit of cricket as it relates to the playing game, and one of the lasting memories I have is of Rod Marsh calling back Derek Randall in the Centenary Test. But in many ways what's more important is cricket's capacity to reach across all ages, all cultures and all socio-economic groups. From a personal point of view, I was a young South African who had been raised in a school that was 100 per cent white, during that dreadful era of apartheid, and yet I was able to leave the country because of cricket. My dad was very keen that I got out of the place as soon as possible; he didn't want me to bring children up in that environment. So I took his advice and moved straight after I left school.

First I went to England, and then in 1968 I toured the world with an International XI. We went to places like Sierra Leone, Kenya, Uganda, Pakistan, India, Ceylon, Malaysia and then home via Bangkok and Hong Kong: places where anyone who had anything to do with apartheid weren't welcome. The cricket world was above that sort of thing. It accepted a young kid, and many like me who came out of that environment, and I now have good friends from every corner of the cricket-playing earth. That to me is the spirit of cricket: what a youngster from any background, race, religion or creed can achieve if he ends up being able to play.

Tony Greig, England 1972–77

Lord Derby, in 1932, said it 'had a great influence of the character of the nation. It has helped to make us a loyal and law-abiding nation.' A year earlier, Lord Harris, on his 80th birthday, wrote a letter to *The Times* advising the young 'to get all the cricket they can. They will never regret it . . . it is more free from anything sordid, anything dishonourable, than any game in the world. To play it keenly, honourably, generously, self-sacrificingly is a moral lesson in itself, and the classroom is God's air and shine.'

This is not merely sepia-tinged poppycock. The identity of cricket has inevitably evolved along with society, but it still exists on a rarefied plane. In 2008, researchers at Loughborough University found that teaching cricket in state schools had a profound effect on children's behaviour. And that of adults. The sportsman's cosy excuse that sport and politics don't mix has sometimes been peddled by cricketers, particularly those who went on rebel tours to South Africa in the dying years of apartheid in the eighties, but as a rule there is a greater individual and collective conscience over such matters. Rarely has that been demonstrated more than by the anguished face of the England captain Nasser Hussain during the interminable Zimbabwe saga at the 2003 World Cup, when England eventually pulled out of their fixture in Zimbabwe and went out of the competition as a result. 'Say that cricket has nothing to do with politics,' wrote John Arlott, 'and you say that cricket has nothing to do with life.'

The Zimbabwe imbroglio dominated the group stages of that World Cup, and reached its peak with a display of unimaginable courage from Andy Flower and Henry Olonga during the match against Namibia, when they wore black armbands to mourn the death of democracy in Zimbabwe. Less renowned but equally inspiring were the actions of those involved in a match between Transvaal and The Rest of South Africa in April 1971. The match was played soon after the government vetoed the selection of two black players, Dik Abed and Owen Williams, for that winter's tour of Australia, and was supposed to celebrate the forming of the Republic of South Africa. After Mike Procter bowled the first ball of the match to Barry Richards, all 22 players walked off the field in protest before resuming the match later on.

ANDY FLOWER AND HENRY OLONGA'S STATEMENT
ZIMBABWE V NAMIBIA, WORLD CUP, HARARE, 10 FEBRUARY 2003

'It is a great honour for us to take the field today to play for Zimbabwe in the World Cup. We feel privileged and proud to have been able to represent our country. We are, however, deeply distressed about what is taking place in Zimbabwe in the midst of the World Cup and do not feel that we can take the field without indicating our feelings in a dignified manner and in keeping with the spirit of cricket.

We cannot in good conscience take to the field and ignore the fact that millions of our compatriots are starving, unemployed and oppressed. We are aware that hundreds of thousands of Zimbabweans may even die in the coming months through a combination of starvation, poverty and Aids. We are aware that many people have been unjustly imprisoned and tortured simply for expressing their opinions about what is happening in the country. We have heard a torrent of racist hate speech directed at minority groups. We are aware that thousands of Zimbabweans are routinely denied their right to freedom of expression. We are aware that people have been murdered, raped, beaten and had their homes destroyed because of their beliefs and that many of those responsible have not been prosecuted.

We are also aware that many patriotic Zimbabweans oppose us even playing in the World Cup because of what is happening.

It is impossible to ignore what is happening in Zimbabwe. Although we are just professional cricketers, we do have a conscience and feelings. We believe that if we remain silent that will be taken as a sign that either we do not care or we condone what is happening in Zimbabwe. We believe that it is important to stand up for what is right.

We have struggled to think of an action that would be appropriate and that would not demean the game we love so much. We have decided that we should act alone without other members of the team being involved because our decision is deeply personal and we did not want to use our senior status to unfairly influence more junior members of the squad. We would like to stress that we greatly respect the ICC and are grateful for all the hard work it has done in bringing the World Cup to Zimbabwe.

In all the circumstances, we have decided that we will each wear a black armband for the duration of the World Cup. In doing so we are mourning the death of democracy in our beloved Zimbabwe. In doing so we are making a silent plea to those responsible to stop the abuse of human rights in Zimbabwe. In doing so, we pray that our small action may help to restore sanity and dignity to our Nation.'

Zimbabwe (340-2) beat Namibia (104-5) by 86 runs (Duckworth/ Lewis method)

South Africa's eventual return to international cricket, in India in November 1991, provided the most joyous example of the spirit of the game. And while it has not always been easy since, with controversy over quotas, the success of Makhaya Ntini has been something to treasure. When he was selected as South Africa's first black Test cricketer against Sri Lanka in 1998, there was inevitable talk that he had not been picked on merit. Ntini's indefatigable excellence soon silenced such slurs, and he became an emblem of a new South Africa.

INDIA V SOUTH AFRICA
1ST ODI, CALCUTTA, 10 NOVEMBER 1991

Most one-day internationals are the day after tomorrow's chip paper, but that certainly was not the case for the three-match series between India and South Africa in November 1991. It was South Africa's first since their post-apartheid readmission and their captain Clive Rice summed up the emotion perfectly when he said: 'I now know how Neil Armstrong felt when he stood on the moon.' The relationship was not reciprocal: the gravity of Rice's experience surely precludes empathy.

The first game was played in a front of a world-record crowd of over 90,000 at Eden Gardens, Calcutta, on 10 November, with Kapil Dev bowling the historic first delivery to Jimmy Cook. The squad was a mix of those who thought they would never play international cricket, like Rice (aged 42), Peter Kirsten (36) and Cook (38), and young men who would go on to star over the next 10 years, most notably Allan Donald (25), Andrew Hudson (26) and Brian McMillan (28).

India won the series 2-1, with Kepler Wessels the stand-out performer for South Africa: he scored half-centuries in every match and replaced Rice as captain for the team's next assignment, the World Cup. It was a rather sour ending to Rice's journey, but the most important thing was that he had made it at all.

South Africa (177-8) lost to India (178-7) by 3 wickets

It is impossible to underestimate cricket's capacity for cultural englightenment and empowerment. Here, as in so much else, we come to Viv Richards. 'It would be hyperbole to assert that Richards empowered Afro-Caribbeans everywhere,' wrote Scyld Berry. 'But by means of his cricket he gave those of them interested in cricket a pride and sense of responsibility – to themselves, to destiny – which they had never known before.'

Richards's pride did not just manifest itself in traditional displays of masculinity. When the West Indies squeezed home by two wickets in a scorching final Test against Pakistan in Barbados in 1987–88, thus preserving their long unbeaten run in Test series, the man who hit the winning runs, Winston Benjamin, came back to the dressing room to one of the more unexpected sights. 'When I saw our captain crying in the dressing room at the end of the game, I realised how much it meant to him,' Benjamin said. 'To see the great Viv Richards in tears made me realise what cricket meant to him and how important this win was for West Indies.'

Before Richards there was Frank Worrell, West Indies' first black captain and an indisputably great man who, as *Wisden* noted, 'had done more than any of his countrymen to bind together the new nations of the Caribbean'. Worrell's influence, on the field at least, was most evident in the 1960–61 series in Australia, when he and his opposite number Richie Benaud's pact to invest in attacking cricket manifested itself in a glorious contest that included the first Tied Test and, at the end of the series, a a ticker-tape thank you as they drove through Melbourne.

Cricket also served to bind together regions and countries during or in the aftermath of war, providing the gentle comfort of the familiar and also the intangible feeling of humanity at its very strongest.

BERT CHEETHAM BOWLS TO LEN HUTTON
ENGLAND V AUSTRALIA, 1ST VICTORY TEST, LORD'S, 19 MAY 1945

In cricket, F/O usually means follow-on, but the language and the landscape were a little different during the Victory Tests of 1945, a series of five three-day matches between England and an Australian Services team that were hastily arranged after the end of the war. Here F/O meant Flying Officer, and the averages for the series included the rank of each player: F/O Keith Miller, Sgt C. G. Pepper, Flt-Lt D. K. Carmody and so on.

The series began at Lord's on 19 May, less than two weeks after VE Day. The matches were not given official status – mainly because Australia were concerned that their squad had only one player with previous Test experience, W/O Lindsay Hassett – yet they were palpably of Test standard. And they launched a bright, shining superstar: 25-year-old Keith Miller, who lorded over the series like the colossus we would soon know. He struck a regal 105 in the first Test at Lord's and ended the series with 514 runs, almost 100 more than anyone else. 'I firmly believe he is destined to become one of the great men of Australian cricket,' wrote Norman Preston in *Wisden*. 'The mere swing of his bat announces his class,' purred the *Guardian*.

Australia won that first Test by six wickets with only two balls to spare, in what the *Guardian* described as 'one of the most exciting finishes ever seen on a cricket ground'. They twice led a series that would end 2–2. For those who have never been involved in war it is extremely difficult to imagine the impact the series had – not just through the comforting sight of cricket being played, but that the matches were infused with such positive cricket alongside the goodwill and hope that inevitably coursed through them. 'Above everything else,' said *Wisden*, 'the cricket provided enjoyment for all kinds of people seeking relaxation after six years of total war.'

Perhaps the most touching story of all concerned the Australian all-rounder Graham Williams, who had been a prisoner in Germany for four years, during which time he taught blinded victims how to read braille. He had been free for less than a fortnight when he walked out to a full house at Lord's. 'He was given a great ovation that compares with anything ever given Bradman, Lillee or Richards,' recalled Miller. 'But it was not the sort of clapping and cheering that greets a hundred. This is different. Everyone stood up. They all knew about Graham's captivity. He was a big fella, but he was gaunt from his experience, and he just walked round for a while as if in a trance.'

England (267 & 294) lost to Australia by (455 & 107-4) by six wickets

MAHELA JAYAWARDENE

Generally the spirit has been pretty good in world cricket for the last seven or eight years; we've had very few problems with players and teams. For me, one thing that really highlighted the spirit of cricket was the reaction to the Tsunami in 2004. The way the cricketing community got together was just amazing. All the matches played in Melbourne and various other places; the Federation of International Cricketers' Associations (FICA) organised so many events all over the world and raised funds for the affected people. For so many people to go out of their way to help showed great spirit.

Playing the first Test at Galle after it was devastated by the Tsunami, against England in 2007, was very emotional. We had to do that because Galle had been such a traditional venue of Sri Lankan cricket and what happened in the Tsunami destroyed the whole town and the ground, and we will never forget the impact it had on so many people. It was a very emotional comeback for professional cricket at Galle and, because of that, my unbeaten double-hundred in that game is one of my proudest innings.

Mahela Jayawardene, Sri Lanka 1997–

More recently, cricket has helped life to return to something resembling normality in the aftermath of various tragedies; examples include the Tsunami and hurricanes Ivan and Jeanne in 2004, the bomb attacks in Mumbai in 2008 and the gun attack on the Sri Lankan team in Lahore in 2009. When Sri Lanka met Pakistan in the World Twenty20 final three months later, Andrew Miller wrote on Cricinfo: 'Sport's great gift for reinvention has delivered a contest that flicks two fingers at the perpetrators of the Lahore atrocity, and proves that – without wishing to overload the sentiment – the human spirit cannot be crushed by cold calculation.'

ALISON MITCHELL

The moment that encapsulates the spirit of cricket to me occurred in Chennai in 2008. England had spent a week at home, pondering whether to return to India following the shocking terrorist attacks in Mumbai, which left more than 150 people dead. India was in a state of national mourning, and the decision to continue the Test tour felt as much about supporting the people of India as fulfilling a cricketing commitment.

I had been covering the one-day internationals for BBC Radio and so returned with the tour party for the Tests, the first of which had been rearranged from Mumbai (Sachin Tendulkar's home city) to Chennai. India were set the fourth-highest total to win in Test history but Tendulkar's century was a masterclass in serenity.

When he came out to join Yuvraj Singh, the match was still tilted in England's favour. He combined concentration with majestic strokeplay to inch India towards their unlikely target.

As an extraordinary win became a distinct reality, the crowd in the Chepauk Stadium began to swell. The screaming and shouting in the stands in front of our commentary box started to reach fever pitch as Tendulkar approached his hundred, and India inched towards their target. When the moment came, it was truly stirring. On 99 and needing four to win, Tendulkar brought up his hundred and won the match with one sweep to the fine-leg boundary.

His celebrations – and that of the crowd - were unbridled; a huge outpouring of emotion, not only for his own achievement but, as a Mumbaiker, for providing a unifying force for the Indian people in such dark times. His press conference afterwards was one of the more emotional I've witnessed. He immediately dedicated his century to all those affected by the Mumbai attacks, acknowledging that while winning a cricket match is of little comfort to those who had lost loved ones, he and his teammates would do everything they could to try to give the people of India something to smile about.

Alison Mitchell is a reporter on Test Match Special

As well as its restorative function, cricket has shown an equal ability to explore new territory and spread its gospel. The first tour was nearly 150 years ago, while the game has always reached unexpected places. Richie Benaud is the patron of the Florida Cricket Club, while a letter to *The Times* in 1950 painted a charming picture of cricket matches in Corfu at the turn of the 20th century. 'They took place on the picturesque parade ground between the lofty citadel and the arcaded town, sometimes in the presence of high dignitaries such as the Governor, the Commandant, the Bishop and priests in their high hats, as well as *evzones* in their fustanellas and British blue-jackets and marines. Sometimes an officer would come into bat in uniform, handing his sword to the umpire to hold during his innings.'

In British sport, La Manga is best known as the place where Paul Gascoigne melted down after being omitted from England's 1998 World Cup squad, but it was also the venue for Cricket España's celebration of 100 years of cricket in 2009. On the subject of football, the north-east of England was always seen as a place that produced footballers and very few other sportsmen, but after Durham attained first-class county status in 1992 it became increasingly apparent that there was an equal passion for cricket. Durham's ascent from bottom of the table in their first two seasons to champions in the last two is the ultimate endorsement of the extraordinary work of their coach Geoff Cook: after an original investment in a number of experienced professionals, Durham began to reap the fruit of the academy that was run by Cook. After some extremely difficult moments – they did not win a single game in the 1996 County Championship – their patient approach was to be rewarded with the emergence of the likes of Steve Harmison, Paul Collingwood and Graham Onions. Back-to-back championships in 2008 and 2009 provided the perfect pay-off.

GEORGE PARR'S TEAM SET OUT ON THE FIRST MAJOR TOUR
7 SEPTEMBER 1859

The modern England team travels to most corners of the globe, yet is it one of the few continents that they do not visit – America – that was the subject of the very first overseas tour. On 7 September 1859, a side of 12 professionals put together by the former Surrey bowler William Pickering set off on a 15-day crossing to Canada and the USA to play five games. They won all their games handsomely, although for a couple the players were split between both teams.

The tour was not without controversy: on the train journey from Montreal to New York, John Lillywhite and George Parr fell out. Lillywhite had a device for making and printing scorecards but, to the exasperation of the team, it kept getting lost. Parr 'in plain language consigned both Lillywhite and his contraption to an unmentionable place'.

There was an incident in an Irish bar, when a local pointed a gun at Julius Caesar, with the police eventually called to calm things down. Financially the trip was a triumph, with each player making £90, and the crowds were unexpectedly good. Two years later the English professionals went to Australia, and cricket has been exploring new frontiers ever since.

The squad was: Bob Carpenter, William Caflyn, Tom Lockyer, John Wisden, H. H. Stephenson, George Parr, John Grundy, Julius Caesar, Tom Hayward, John Jackson, Alfred Diver and John Lillywhite.

Those who feel that the spirit of cricket has creaked under the pressures of the modern world would have to acknowledge that women's cricket offers a counter view. After decades of repression, the development of the women's game has offered copious evidence of the spirit of the game: from playing at Lord's for the first time in 1976, when girls were finally allowed, through to Claire Taylor's richly deserved inclusion as one of *Wisden*'s Five Cricketers of the Year in 2009. And to further stress the entirely individual nature of the spirit of cricket, Richie Benaud of all people was accused of sexism in a letter to the *Guardian* in 1981. His crime? To suggest that 'schoolboys' could learn much from David Gower's strokeplay.

Benaud is arguably the greatest broadcaster in the history of sport, never mind cricket, and the wit and literary tradition that courses through cricket in the media is a gift that keeps on giving. 'It's hard to imagine a sport that indulges the writer more than cricket,' wrote Sambit Bal in the first edition of *Cricinfo Magazine*. 'It is the grandest of all sports: endlessly fascinating; rich in artistry; full of cerebral and emotional possibilities, subtlety and grace; but hardly lacking in thrill, pace, athleticism and physical combat. Its duration allows character to be revealed, fortunes to twist and turn, and writers to craft fine prose. No wonder cricket boasts a body of literature unrivalled by that of any other sport.'

Cricket treasures its writers in a way that other sports often do not; during the Centenary Test of 1980, play stopped to honour the last broadcast of the great John Arlott. Arlott didn't play the game to any great level, but he'll always be remembered as the Voice of Cricket. With his soft Hampshire burr he gave the listener the sense of being in the best seat in the house: as Brian Johnston said: 'You could smell bat oil when he spoke.' After working in a planning office, a mental hospital, and as a policeman, Arlott came late to cricket commentary, but he was born for the unique properties of radio, and his last stint in the Test commentary box – during the Centenary Test at Lord's in 1980 – overshadowed the match itself. As Arlott uttered his last words, play stopped as the whole ground stood to applaud him. He died in 1991, and in a *Wisden Cricket Monthly* obituary David Frith wrote: 'A great English oak has come down, and the landscape seems bare.'

Before Arlott there was Neville Cardus, a humble, anti-establishment man who revolutionised sportswriting by rejecting the accepted way of doing things; Matthew Engel described him as 'an artist of devastating originality'.

Cricket's writing fraternity have also provided unwitting moments of the sort of absurdity in which cricket unashamedly revels. In 1983, Henry Blofeld was reporting on an underwhelming match between Surrey and Essex for the *Guardian*. With an hour to go, and an evening function demanding his urgent presence, Blofeld filed his report and instructed the sports desk to fill in Surrey's score, reasoning they would lose a couple of wickets at most. They were 14 all out.

Similarly, it is hard to imagine another sport in which a player would walk out of a press conference because he had a taxi waiting to take him to see *Anything Goes*, as the England captain David Gower did at Lord's in 1989. Or one that would produce as infectious a calypso as 'those little pals of mine', Lord Beginner's tribute to the West Indian spin twins, Sonny Ramadhin and Alf Valentine, after they had thrashed England at Lord's in 1950.

'THOSE LITTLE PALS OF MINE'
WEST INDIES V ENGLAND, 2ND TEST, LORD'S,
24–9 JUNE 1950

'Cricket lovely Cricket, At Lord's where I saw it; Cricket lovely Cricket, At Lord's where I saw it; Yardley tried his best But Goddard won the test. They gave the crowd plenty fun; Second Test and West Indies won.

Chorus: With those two little pals of mine Ramadhin and Valentine.

The King was there well attired, So they started with Rae and Stollmeyer; Stolly was hitting balls around the boundary; But Wardle stopped him at twenty. Rae had confidence, So he put up a strong defence; He saw the King was waiting to see, So he gave him a century.

Chorus: With those two little pals of mine Ramadhin and Valentine.

West Indies first innings total was three-twenty-six Just as usual When Bedser bowled Christiani The whole thing collapsed quite easily; England then went on, And made one-hundred-fifty-one; West Indies then had two-twenty lead And Goddard said, 'That's nice indeed.'

Chorus: With those two little pals of mine Ramadhin and Valentine.

Yardley wasn't broken-hearted When the second innings started; Jenkins was like a target, Getting the first five in his basket. But Gomez broke him down, While Walcott licked them around; He was not out for one-hundred and sixty-eight, Leaving Yardley to contemplate.

Chorus: The bowling was superfine Ramadhin and Valentine.

West Indies was feeling homely, Their audience had them happy. When Washbrook's century had ended, West Indies voices all blended.Hats went in the air.

They jumped and shouted without fear; So at Lord's was the scenery Bound to go down in history.

Chorus: After all was said and done Second Test and the West Indies won!'

West Indies (326 & 425-6 dec) beat England 151 & 274 by 326 runs

It is even harder to imagine another sport in which a cat would receive an obituary.

Peter the Cat was honoured in the 1965 edition of *Wisden*, having been the Lord's cat for 12 years from his birth in 1952. 'He was a cat of great character and loved publicity,' noted *Wisden*, '[whose] sleek brown form could often be seen prowling on the field of play when crowds were biggest.' He even lent his name to a recent anthology, *Peter the Lord's Cat and Other Unexpected Obituaries from* Wisden.

The spirit of cricket might be evident through the *Wisden Cricketers' Almanack*, the 'bible of cricket' that is given all the reverence such a phrase implies. Woe betide the person who damages another's yellow jacket. *Wisden* has an almost unmanageable authority – notice the amount of times, evident in this book, that it is quoted as gospel – but retains the keenest eye for cricket's kookiness. In the 1995 edition, for example, we were told that a six hit by Graeme Hick flew through an open window and struck a spectator named Doris Day.

A similar reverence is afforded *Test Match Special*, the BBC

Radio broadcasts that cover everything from cricket to cakes and all points in between. *TMS*'s random digressions, outstanding analysis and often schoolboy humour have made it a uniquely British institution, and an addictive one: those at the ground or watching on TV frequently supplement the experience with the *Test Match Special* commentary.

'JUST DIDN'T QUITE GET HIS LEG OVER'
ENGLAND V WEST INDIES, 5TH TEST, THE OVAL,
8–12 AUGUST 1991

In the aftermath of Brian Johnston and Jonathan Agnew's wonderfully infectious fit of the giggles on *Test Match Special* in 1991, the only two people not smiling were Johnston and Agnew. Both were furious at their lack of professionalism, but would soon come to love a moment that defines *TMS*'s tittersome appeal more than any other.

After England had been dismissed for 419, Johnston and Agnew were reviewing the innings. The seventh wicket down was Ian Botham, who was out hit wicket after failing to hurdle the stumps when he was knocked off balance by a short ball from Curtly Ambrose. 'Just just didn't quite get his leg over,' mumbled Agnew mischievously. Johnson attempted to carry on, even saying 'Aggers, do stop it', but was powerless to resist and started wheezing deliriously when he struggled to relay the suddenly hilarious fact that David Lawrence had hit a four over the wicketkeeper's head. Johnston, still in the throes of laughter, then pleaded: 'Aggers, for goodness sake stop it!'

Agnew tried to resume normal service, only to be reduced to an uncontrollable cackle before he could get his first word out. They recovered their poise within a minute, but they had inadvertently provided one of the great sport commentary moments. And one of the warmest. Try listening to it without smiling, and then surrender to the inevitable, just as Aggers and Johnners did.

England (419 & 146-5) beat West Indies (176 & 385) by 5 wickets

Those fans at the ground, or watching elsewhere, also make significant contributions to the spirit of cricket. Probably the most obvious example is in the generous ovations accorded to triumphant opponents. When Pakistan won a coronary-inducer by 12 runs at Chennai in 1998–99, the first Test between the sides for nearly a decade, they were applauded off by a devastated local crowd. Harold Larwood received a rousing ovation when he made 98 as a nightwatchman in the final Bodyline Test at Sydney. The goodwill of the 2005 Ashes was evident in the English response to Shane Warne, particularly the stirring applause for his 600th Test wicket and the chants of 'We wish you were English' on that heady final day at The Oval. And when the 42-year-old Bobby Simpson came out of retirement to lead a Packer-ravaged Australia in the West Indies in 1977–78, he was given a spine-shivering standing ovation by 24,000 in Trinidad when he came out to bat in the first Test.

Fan interaction was even more evident when Merv Hughes was conducting crowds to follow his absurd callisthenics, a cult that started by accident when Dean Jones pointed out to Hughes that hundreds of people behind him were mimicking his attempts to keep loose between deliveries. Fans have also been known to have a direct impact upon the outcome of a game. There was the famous mop-up of the waterlogged outfield at The Oval, which allowed Derek Underwood to bowl England to victory. When a county championship match between Sussex and Gloucestershire in 1947 was delayed by a fire in the South Stand at Hove, *The Times* reported that fire crews were aided by 'many volunteers with pickaxes and choppers'.

Crowds can also contribute to the kind of atmosphere that singes a place in the memory. A personal favourite occurred at Trinidad in 1994, when England were bowled out for 46, but similar examples are dotted throughout history. The rhythm of cricket, allowing the tension to build between each delivery, only aids such an atmosphere.

46 ALL OUT
WEST INDIES V ENGLAND, 3RD TEST, TRINIDAD, 25–30 MARCH 1994

Geoffrey Boycott might not seem an expert on excitement, yet few questioned him when he described this as the most exciting passage of play he'd ever witnessed. When Curtly Ambrose blew England away on the fourth evening in Trinidad, leaving them 40-8, it was about so much more than the admittedly thrilling sight of

THE SPIRIT OF CRICKET

stumps flying all over the place. The atmosphere in the Queen's Park Oval was extraordinary: frighteningly primal, and a collective demonstration of almost demented pride in the face of apparently inevitable defeat.

Ambrose was blessed with a force and a rage that enabled him to script some of Test cricket's most memorable collapses – he had taken 7-1 against Australia 14 months earlier – and that, allied to the intense concentration and raucous celebration of the crowd, left a young England side helpless.

They had needed 194 for a stirring victory, but would get only a quarter of that. They lost their captain Mike Atherton to the first ball and were soon 5-3. When Ambrose sent Graham Thorpe's off stump into the next postal district with the final delivery of the day, Thorpe's glassy-eyed bewilderment said it all. England had not just been beaten by Ambrose, or by the West Indies cricket team. They had been beaten by the West Indies.

West Indies (252 & 269) beat England (328 & 46) by 147 runs

In such situations, cricket goes beyond sport and into the realms of art. The picturesque nature of so many grounds, from the Adelaide Oval to Eden Gardens in Kolkata, captures the spirit of cricket without recourse to words. Anyone who has experienced Festival Week at Canterbury may have a similar feeling. 'The annual Canterbury Week, when the spirit of cricket pervades the very air one breathes . . .' began a report in *The Times* in 1930. Canterbury is an example of grounds whose beauty provides more than just a visually alluring backdrop: Colonel A. C. 'Jacko'

Watson, Learie Constantine, Jim Smith and Carl Hooper are the only men to have ever hit a six over the famous Lime Tree, the jewel in Canterbury's crown until high winds felled it in 2005. 'It received more gushingly fulsome obits than those for a minor royal,' noted Frank Keating in the *Guardian*.

In a *Guardian* report of a match between Leicestershire and Lancashire in 1920, their correspondent, 'Cricketer', went off on imperious digression to this end.

Why should cricket lovers not pay due homage to the setting in which Nature in her grateful moods places the summer pastime? Why must we be eternally seeking in cricket for a wherewithal to unloose mere combative energy? Let the play be what it will, is not the warm sunshine worth sitting in, and does not the motion of the men in white soothe like the rhythm of soft music? There is poetry in cricket as well as stern conflict. Let us indulge it now and again, even at the cost of shouting our side home. On this Leicester cricket field, so redolent of the village green, one is far away from your modern gladiatorial contests set in the midst of a hoarse multitude. Here, something in the very air conjures up the ancient spirit of cricket, the Hambledon grace and companionable ease.

SAM MENDES

In 1997–98 I toured India with Harold Pinter's side, the Gaieties, and we played a game in Delhi that signifies the spirit of cricket to me. Three particular incidents were just wonderful. It was New Year's Day 1998; we'd been up all night and gathered hungover in the lobby at 9 o'clock to find that the bus wasn't there. By 10 o'clock it wasn't there, and by 11 o'clock it wasn't there. The game was starting at 11.15. Finally it arrived, so we all piled on the bus sullenly before it started up. It then drove precisely 30 yards round the corner to the ground. We were met by Bishen Bedi, who was playing on the opposing side that day. We tried to explain that we'd waited two hours for a bus to drive us 30 yards, and he said simply, with a huge smile, 'This is India'.

We started to play, and I was batting at number 3, feeling pretty good about myself as I nudged a few runs off the great Bishen Bedi. Then my friend, the actor Jonathan Cake, came in to bat. Bedi was floating up, in his inimitable way, these beautiful, drifting, dipping deliveries that you would hear fizzing in the air. You think it's there to hit until it suddenly dips and turns. In the course of one over, Johnny played every shot in the MCC coaching manual – and he missed the ball every time. At the end of the over he strode calmly down the wicket to pat down the pitch in a semi-pro manner, and Bedi walked up to him and said: 'My friend, you have hit me everywhere and nowhere.' One of the great lines. It caused an enormous amount of hilarity, both at the time and when the rest of the team heard about it.

I got 40-odd, which I was very happy with, and Mike Simkins, an actor who went on to write *Fatty Batter*, came in at number 8. Everyone was so excited because Bedi was bowling; for my generation he was a major figure. Mike went in with a look of utter determination on his face, and the second ball he attempted was the most flamboyant, Pietersenesque reverse-sweep at Bedi that I've ever seen. He twisted himself into a pretzel, turning round so far that he ended up getting caught at first slip. The standing ovation he received from the entire team as he walked back to the pavilion has to rank as the greatest-ever ovation for a second-ball duck. It was triumphant: the fact that he had planned this and then nearly given himself a hernia as he tried to essay the shot. It was definitely the champagne moment; in fact it was the highlight of the tour.

As anyone who has toured India will tell you, there's an incredible friendship. At the end of the match – they slaughtered us of course – we were all sharing a curry and talking cricket, and I recall looking across the outfield at the dusty haze of late afternoon and thinking, It is a truly great sport. That's the reason for sport, to bring people together: to watch, to play, to tal̶ ̶d to share stories and cultures. In terms of a sport that has bee̶ ̶ ̶t of my life, that was a defining moment.

Sam Mendes is the Academ
American Beaut̶
Revolut̶

A similar theme was struck by Norman Preston in his editor's notes for the 1960 *Wisden Cricketers' Almanack*. 'The English season of 1959 will be remembered by all lovers of cricket as one that brought a renascence to the game, especially in county circles,' Preston wrote. 'It was a wonderful summer with days on end of glorious sunshine and one in deep contrast to the miserable wet days of several preceding years.'

If the sun is at the mercy of a higher authority, then cricket's community has been inevitably keen to preserve that beauty which can be controlled. That was manifest in the brouhaha over reports in 2009 that Lord's was to be redeveloped at a cost of £400 million. Such reactions are not new. In 1906, a piece in the *Observer* suggested that 'Lord's and tradition long ago parted company. The public no doubt benefited by the divorce; it got its huge mound stand to command a bird's-eye view of the game; it secured more refreshment bars and trifling considerations.' At the same time it mourned the 'passing of the poetry from Lord's'. Poetry is still evident in the humble scene from the village green, a never-ending well into which we can dip and find the spirit of the game.

If such things take cricket into the realms of art, then the experience of watching the game can equally embrace comedy. The prime example is the peculiar – and as yet medically unrecognised – disease that is being an England cricket supporter. For a team who are occasionally very good and often worse than mediocre, England inspire the most comical among their supporters. Anybody who has broken the ice with a guilty snigger as yet another England wicket falls will know the feeling. For cricket fans of a certain age, growing up was all about insecurity, self-doubt and England batting collapses. In reverse order.

The Macbethian insistence of referring to the 'South Australian ground' rather than Adelaide, the scene of England's traumatic collapse in the 2006–07 Ashes, offered a new spin on that theme. And while events from the South Australian ground have been expunged from many a memory, most fans can recall other famous England collapses in all their grisly details. Those fans are invariably self-confessed nerds – 'cricket tragics' is the vogue term – and such a trait is also in evidence among many players. For example, when Muttiah Muralitharan signed for Lancashire, his new teammate Ian Austin was staggered by the extent of his knowledge of the minutiae of each player's career.

Another Lancastrian, Mike Atherton, was discussing the spirit of cricket in *The Times* in 2009 when he offered an enchanting reminder of the oft-forgotten fact that most of the great players start as starry-eyed fans, just like the rest of us.

A young Lancastrian [he describes himself], obsessed with the game. Playing the dice game Owzthat for hours on end with nobody for company and still able to remember the Lancashire team that adorned the scorebook: Lloyd (D), Wood, Pilling, Lloyd (C), Hayes, Engineer, Hughes, Simmons, Lever, Lee, Shuttleworth. Then, later, hitting a ball in a sock tied to a washing line for hours so that no grass ever grew there in the summer. Was it possible to be more excited about a game?

If, as a child, you did not fritter away at least one whole day replaying a Test match between the 1948 Australians and the 1980s West Indies with Lambourne Games' 'International Cricket', your life cannot be said to have been fulfilled.

The youngster's devotion to scoring while at the game is another example, while cricket also offers infinite scope for man's true best friend: compiling a list. There is nary a cricket fan who has not, at some stage, wasted ten minutes compiling an XI – an all-time World XI, perhaps, or an England duffers XI – and not regretted a second of it.

An offshoot of being a cricket tragic is the kind of eccentric behaviour that lives in the memory, whether it's Jack Russell wringing 20 cups of tea from every teabag, Alan Knott's refusal to have meat and cheese in the same meals, or Dickie Bird turning up four hours early for Tests. Here, again, is the paradox with the spirit of cricket: to many it is vital to embrace cricket as part of life – 'What they know of cricket who only cricket know?' as C. L. R. James said – whereas a childlike obsession with the game is an equally powerful demonstration of its spirit.

DICKIE BIRD

I can honestly say that in my era, when I was a Test umpire, I never had one moment's problem from a single professional throughout the cricket world. They were all marvellous to me. The game was always played in the right way. The one person who really summed up the spirit of cricket was Michael Brearley; I don't have to think about it for a second. He was a credit to his profession, and on top of that I rate him as one of the finest captains I've ever had the pleasure of being out in the middle alongside.

All sport should be played within the spirit of the game. When I was a young colt at Yorkshire that was instilled in me by Maurice Leyland and Arthur Mitchell: they were great players but also wonderful gentleman. Play hard, by all means, but play within the Laws and spirit of the game. We must stress this, with all sports. For example, my last Test match, between England and India at Lord's in 1996, was played with a wonderful spirit. It started off well for me when both sides lined up to give me a guard of honour and the crowd game me a standing ovation as I came on to the field, and that was a tremendous honour for me. It was very moving, and then I had to give Mike Atherton LBW in the first over – and he was the one who had arranged for the players to line up and applaud me. It was an unbelievable occasion for me.

Dickie Bird scored 3,314 first-class runs at 20.71 for Yorkshire between 1956 and 1964, and later umpired 66 Tests

Those who embrace a life beyond cricket can still demonstrate those obsessions. Bob Willis's love of Bob Dylan is well known, while that fine Indian spinner Dilip Doshi claims to have listened to literally no music other than the Rolling Stones for the past 40 years. Hero worship is also evident within the game, sometimes comically so, as was shown by a contest between the South African fast bowler Andre Nel and his idol Allan Donald in 2001. Nel had been told by his crackpot coach Ray Jennings to bomb Donald with short stuff. When he struck Donald with a short one, forcing him to retire hurt, Nel burst into tears. 'His hero ducks into a short one so what does he do? He goes and sobs over him like a girl guide,' sniffed Jennings. 'I told him to pin him with the next ball and pin him again until he didn't get up.'

A more poetic example of hero worship came when Arthur Mailey bowled the great Victor Trumper and said he 'felt like the boy who killed a dove'. Another Australian, Sid Barnes, got himself out on 234 against England at Sydney in 1946–47 so that he would not exceed Don Bradman's score in the same game. The two had added 405 for the fifth wicket and were both on 234 when Bradman fell to Norman Yardley. Barnes did the honourable thing in the next over from Alec Bedser. 'I don't think I should have got more than Bradman,' he said simply. When Jack Hobbs was married in 1906, there was surprise that he had not invited Tom Hayward, his opening partner with Surrey. 'Although I had been associated with him for two cricket seasons, I had not lost that feeling of awe of him,' said Hobbs. 'I did not think that the wedding would be grand enough for him or that I should be able to accommodate him in the style that his position warranted.'

As a child, Viv Richards says he was more preoccupied with the three Ws – Weekes, Worrell and Walcott – than the three Rs: reading, 'ritin and 'rithmetic. Colin Cowdrey vividly recalled his 'private world of intense excitement' when, as a young boy, he saw his hero Wally Hammond come out to bat at Lord's. 'He was not a cricketer walking out to bat but a god gracing the afternoon with his presence, and the effect on me was profound.'

You do not need to be among the crowd to be a spectator. When the West Indies' captain Richie Richardson made a fine century at Sydney in 1992–93, it was almost secondary to his role as an awestruck observer as Brian Lara lashed his way to a scintillating 277, his maiden Test century and an innings that announced cricket's latest genius. 'I can hardly remember my hundred,' he said. 'It was difficult playing and being a spectator at the same time.'

On the same ground in 2006–07, Australia sealed an Ashes whitewash against England, and the former England coach David Lloyd recalls scooting down from his Sky commentary position at the end of the match to take a personal photo of the two champions, Glenn McGrath and Shane Warne, walking off arm in arm at the end of their final Test. McGrath and Warne were the very men who cost Lloyd the chance of an Ashes victory in 1997, but the game has always seen beyond the parochial. Lloyd's photograph also signified a respect for the history of the game, something that cricket holds to an unusual degree.

MICHAEL HUSSEY
AUSTRALIA V WEST INDIES, 1ST TEST, BRISBANE, 3–6 NOVEMBER 2005

After 20 Tests Michael Hussey averaged a Bradmanesque 84.80. He scored an Australian-record 15,313 first-class runs before making his Test debut. The bald statistics suggest the smoothest transition; a remorseless run-machine barely noticing the step up. Yet the truth could hardly have been more different, for Hussey's debut Test innings was among the most tortured in the game's history.

The reason it was so tortured was precisely *because* of the game's history. The Baggy Green may have fit snugly in a physical sense, but Hussey could not get his head round the idea of wearing it. The story that he saw his first ball through clouds of tears may or may not be apocryphal, but he did admit that he was an 'emotional wreck' and that he could hardly feel his legs after hearing 'that bloody national anthem'. Hussey scored 1 from 14 balls before top-edging a pull to the wicketkeeper.

He would quickly find his form, lacing centuries in his second, third and fifth Tests, but Hussey's travails are an example of the extraordinary reverence afforded the Baggy Green by modern Australian cricketers. The cult started in the nineties, when Mark Taylor and Steve Waugh began to prioritise it as the symbol of the all-conquering teams over which they presided. Taylor made sure it was presented to every debutant by a former great in a pre-match ceremony, and that the entire team wore it during the first session in the field. Matthew Hayden called those who had played Test cricket for Australia the 'brothers of the Baggy Green'. When Michael Clarke moved within sight of a gorgeous debut century in India in 2004, he pointedly discarded his helmet in favour of his cap.

The Baggy Green began to acquire an almost mystical quality. Phillip Hughes keeps his in a pouch in his wardrobe, checking on it every morning like a dutiful son. 'I even smell it sometimes.' The last one worn by Donald Bradman went for nearly £200,000 at auction. 'There's no price tag on it,' said Steve Waugh. 'It's my most prized possession.' It is not to all tastes – when the entire Australian squad sported the cap at Wimbledon while supporting their countryman Pat Rafter in the men's singles final of 2001, Mike Atherton described it as 'enough to make you puke' – but, as with the deification of the All Black rugby jersey, it is hard not to be moved at some level by such overwhelming patriotism and respect for the game's history. And with Australia's record over the last 20 years, who is to argue with their methods?

'As far as the team is concerned,' Waugh said, 'the traditions we uphold are an important element used to develop a sense of pride, camaraderie and high morale that hopefully will give us a mental toughness when we are challenged. Not only do we embrace tradition, we feel an obligation to set new ones to hand on.'

Not everyone agrees. 'It is a $5 bit of cloth,' says Ian Chappell. 'I haven't got one, haven't had one since the day I finished. I don't need to look at an Australian cap to remind me of what I did.'

In Chappell's day it meant little: Bill Lawry wore his while cleaning his pigeon's nest, while Bill Ponsford used his to protect his hair while he was painting. The players were given a new cap for each tour, but now players are limited to just one during the career. If they need to change it because of wear and tear, they must sign a statutory declaration before it can be replaced.

For the likes of Waugh and Ricky Ponting, replacing the Baggy Green is not an option. Waugh agonised like the owner of a sick pet over whether to have some remedial work done to his at the beginning of the last decade, while Ponting's, though as robust and tough as the man himself, needed some treatment at the start of 2010. It's something you cannot imagine in England. Which makes it rather ironic that the caps are produced by a company called Albion.

Australia (435 & 283-2 dec) beat West Indies (210 & 129) by 379 runs

There is a fascination with and respect for the heritage of the game that is rare and endearing. It might manifest itself in the copying of another's technique or style. Andrew Caddick famously aped Richard Hadlee's bowling action, while Geoff Boycott – not exactly everybody's idea of the spirit of cricket made flesh – describes a nice moment when, during an innings in Australia in 1978–79, he congratulated himself that a cover-drive was 'just like Leonard', a tribute to another great opening batsman, Len Hutton.

14 MARCH

Beware the Ides of March and, if you are a cricket fan, be thankful for the day before. Coincidentally 14 March has provided five of cricket's most unforgettable incidents, making it comfortably the most striking in this particular calendar.

Ordering them is impossible, except perhaps chronologically. First comes the most famous single over of them all, in Bridgetown in 1980–81, when Michael Holding started at top gear to Geoff Boycott and then cranked it up even higher before sending Boycott's off stump flying with the final delivery. Chris Old, Boycott's England teammate, said he 'had the look of a man who had seen a monster'.

West Indies were apparently affected by demons when they collapsed to lose the 1996 World Cup semi-final against Australia. From 165 for two, chasing just 208, West Indies fell apart completely against Shane Warne and Damien Fleming, losing by five runs.

That was as good as 14 March got for Australia. In 1999 and 2001 they suffered the extremely rare embarrassment of watching two batsmen bat all day: first Brian Lara and Jimmy Adams for West Indies, then V. V. S. Laxman and Rahul Dravid for India. Both set up unforgettable victories for the home side.

Then, in a bizarre reversal of that Jamaica game, Steve Harmison bowled the West Indies out for just 47 in 2004, taking 7 for 12. It was a false dawn for Harmison, if not England: it set them on the way to six consecutive series victories for the first time since the 19th century, culminating in the 2005 Ashes.

Then again, not everyone will remember 14 March fondly. In 1986, in his first match upon returning to the Caribbean after suffering a particularly nasty broken nose at the hands of Malcolm

Marshall, Mike Gatting had his thumb broken by Barbados's Vibert Greene in a tour match and missed the next two Tests.

It can also manifest itself in more curious ways. It is a little-known fact that, if you pause time at 8.22 p.m. on a Friday night, at least one group of people in a bar or pub are attempting to name the 29 players who played for England in the 1989 Ashes. (For the record, we got 27, and the full list is: Mike Atherton, Kim Barnett, Ian Botham, Chris Broad, David Capel, Nick Cook, Tim Curtis, Phil DeFreitas, Graham Dilley, John Emburey, Neil Foster, Angus Fraser, Mike Gatting, Graham Gooch, David Gower, Eddie Hemmings, Alan Igglesden, Paul Jarvis, Allan Lamb, Devon Malcolm, Martyn Moxon, Phil Newport, Derek Pringle, Tim Robinson, Jack Russell, Gladstone Small, Robin Smith, John Stephenson and Chris Tavare.)

The spirit of cricket courses through the game's history in thousands of ways: some unavoidably enormous, some infinitesimal. Whatever happens in the future, that is unlikely to change.

CONCLUSION

The MCG, 26 December 2037. The traditional Boxing Day Ten10 has gone down to the wire. Australia scored 187 for fifteen from their ten overs, with their young captain Alex Heinrich taking advantage of the 50-metre boundaries to blast five sixes in an over. West Indies are 184 for seventeen with one ball remaining when a verbal exchange between Australia's opening bowler Clint 'Slugger' Campbell and the West Indies' batsman Everton Pollard spills over into fisticuffs. Both players are sent off and, when the new batsman Anthony Rodriguez hits the final delivery for four to win the match, his 'up yours' gesture sparks a mass brawl.

Such a dystopian scenario may seem utterly absurd. It almost certainly is. In 20 years' time, we may well look back and chuckle at the current moral panic engulfing cricket because of the increasing primacy of Twenty20. After all, World Series Cricket was apparently going to endanger the Test match. In 1977, Geoffrey Moorhouse outlined his fears in the *Guardian*. 'I've had this sinking feeling ever since returning home last month,' he said. 'It is essentially about a very precious spirit that happens to have been located most intensively in cricket for a hundred years or so. For the first time in my life I can see it vanishing – beneath a cloud of banknotes – unless enough of us is prepared to stand up and tell the mercenaries to bugger off and leave this game alone.'

As long ago as 1906, the *Guardian* lamented the fact that 'County secretaries do not exhale the sweet chivalry of the spirit of cricket . . . it is just the rude spirit of commerce entering into sport to warp the extension of human sympathy, that groundwork of religious instinct which oils the wheels of the world.' Yet while these concerns may not be new, they are on a previously unimaginable scale: the seismic events of the first decade of the 21st century mean that the need for vigilance with regard to the spirit of cricket is as great as ever. 'Unquestionably cricket acquired unimaginable riches in the noughties,' wrote Cricinfo editor Sambit Bal at the end of 2009. 'The coming decade will tell us if the game lost its soul in the bargain.' Bal christened the noughties the Decade of Change. 'Not just any change. But once-in-a-generation Change. Path-altering, future-shaping and game-changing Change. Change so radical and so outrageous that it couldn't have been foreseen, much less planned. Much of it has caught most people unaware, and it has left the world of cricket feeling a mixture of confusion, excitement and apprehension.'

Add that to a society apparently unravelling towards ritual disorder and intent on desecrating that which is sacred in a manner that makes Fred Truemans of us all as we lament what it was like in our day and, for the first time in a long while, perhaps ever, the future of the game feels entirely impossible to predict: it is tantalising, exciting, disconcerting and confusing.

Cricket has generally been a sedate game: unashamedly languorous in nature, a haven of serenity away from the mania of the rat race. Yet that has changed dramatically of late, both on and off the field, with fast scoring and even faster bucks. Consequently, it is almost impossible to know in which direction the game is heading. Even educated guesses are out. Traditionally, looking into cricket's crystal ball has been a fun and whimsical exercise but now it is fraught with concern and confusion. Even Nostradamus would probably ask to phone a friend. Truly, as the Hollywood screenwriter William Goldman famously said, nobody knows anything.

When Cricinfo's editorial team were asked to predict what would happen in the next ten years, there was a flurry of mixed predictions. 'Tired of meaningless fixtures . . . spectators will have deserted Twenty20 by 2019,' said Peter English. 'By 2020, Twenty20s will stand alone,' suggested Andrew Miller. One of the few apparent certainties is that, for richer or even richer, Twenty20 will govern cricket's future. The concern is that cricket will follow the path of football and embrace a reductive greed. The evidence suggests that, even before we consider Twenty20, it already has: in the noughties there were 464 Tests, as compared to 347 in the nineties, and 1,402 one-day internationals (as compared to 933 in the nineties). The bodies and minds of the players, never mind the minds (and the wallets) of the spectators, cannot take it.

It is easy for those in power to preach that they will do right by the game; much harder, as football has demonstrated, to practise it. Yet the likes of IPL chairman Lalit Modi have a very serious moral responsibility to centuries of tradition, one that must be foremost in every single decision they make.

'The most grievous fear is that the Gordon Gekkos running the game will continue to believe that fixture congestion is good, that quantity is more important than quality, that greed is good,' wrote Rob Steen at the turn of the decade. 'Among those of a certain age, paranoia reigns: will our beloved anachronism, the five-day Test, be sacrificed on the altar of artifice and wafer-thin concentration spans?'

The preponderance of Twenty20 is anything but a bitesize concern for those who cherish first-class cricket; who want to see maidens rather than cheerleaders. If one-day cricket was fast food, then the game is now in danger of supersizing itself. Test cricket may be a lyrical, winding sentence in comparison to the txtspk of Twenty20; if so, cricket is reflecting life in its preference for the latter. The *Guardian*'s Andy Bull says he treats Twenty20 as 'a different sport', which gives a whole new meaning to the phrase 'It's not cricket'.

The advent of the IPL and the Champions League suggest that cricket may ape football by having the club rather than the international game as its focus. The emergence of the freelance cricketer, such as Andrew Flintoff and Andrew Symonds, reinforces that perception. Should that be so, there is a particular concern as to how, in a format in which players are currently permitted to represent multiple club sides, each team will acquire a relevant identity. So far the IPL has felt like a novel but ultimately meaningless collection of individual contests – oh look, there's Murali bowling to Gilchrist – without the collective thread which ties it all together. It has no context. List who you think are the ten best players in the world and then try to add their IPL team. If you get more than five, congratulations.

For all that, it would be remiss to paint Twenty20 as an irredeemable evil. It has plenty of the innocence and fun that gets to the core of cricket's Golden Age, and it has already spread the game's gospel in ways that the first-class game never could. If distributed and consumed responsibly – and that, surely, is the most important issue – Twenty20 has so much to offer the game.

'Like nuclear power, it can either save our world or destroy it, change it forever,' wrote Harsha Bhogle. 'And like nuclear power, it needs to be harnessed for the development of the game.'

It cannot match the subtlety of the longer form, particularly in areas such as captaincy and individual duels. Indeed Donald v Atherton in 1998 lasted for over half of an entire Twenty20 innings. But we must be careful with our assumptions: when limited-overs cricket began, few people envisaged that a 50-over cricket match could possess anything like the gravitas of the astonishing World Cup semi-final between Australia and South Africa in 1999.

At the very least, Twenty20 can supply variations on themes like the individual duel. In the final of the World Twenty20 in 2009 between Pakistan and Sri Lanka, the 17-year-old Mohammad Aamer's clinical five-ball defenestration of 32-year-old Tillakaratne

Dilshan, the player of the tournament, in the very first over had a classical coming-of-age quality.

That tournament, and the inaugural World Twenty 20 in South Africa two years earlier, were both enormous fun – particularly in contrast to the hideous, obese 50-over World Cup in the West Indies in 2007 – and offered much else that captured the spirit of cricket. Holland's astonishing victory over England; the charm of a young Indian side triumphing unexpectedly in 2007; the totemic influence of Shahid Afridi, the maverick's maverick, in 2009; the purity of James Foster's wicketkeeping (even if he was dropped afterwards for not scoring enough runs); an extremely agreeable balance between bat and ball; heroism in defeat from the likes of Chris Gayle, against South Africa in 2007; the unprecedented variety of the Sri Lankan spinner Ajantha Mendis, with scarcely a batsman in the world who was truly compos Mendis; the irresistible charisma of Dwayne Bravo; umpteen innovations, most notably the Dilscoop; fielding of such widespread intelligence and athleticism that it would have been unimaginable even ten years ago; and even the success of more orthodox batsmanship from the likes of Younis Khan and Shivnarine Chanderpaul. In a manic, shortened decider against England at the Oval in 2009, it was not power hitting that won the game but the cool accumulation of Chanderpaul and Ramnaresh Sarwan. To the Oval members that will not have been a surprise: Mark Ramprakash had been doing it that way since Twenty20 started in 2003.

By the time this book is published, Afghanistan will have played in the third World Twenty20, a story of enormous romance. For all the concerns, cricket is not exactly in bad shape.

In October 2009, playing for LB Shastri in a Delhi under-16 tournament, the 15-year-old Nitish Rana made 195, adding 349 with Siddharth Sehwag in a partnership which evoked the famous 664-run stand between a Sachin Tendulkar, aged 14, and a 16-year-old Vinod Kambli in their school days.

Rana was within five of a double century when, after a big appeal for caught behind, he was given not out. So he walked. 'I knew I was out,' he said, 'and I did not want to score a double-century with the feeling that I was out.'

In this book, Eoin Morgan, one of England's most lustrous young talents, says the spirit of cricket is something that is passed imperceptibly from one generation to the next. It can only be hoped that this process will continue, and that characters such as Nitish Rana will continue instinctively to understand the game and what it means.

At this precise moment, somewhere a young boy or girl is fixing a poster of Sachin Tendulkar, Ricky Ponting or Claire Taylor to their bedroom wall. Another is out in the back garden, getting throwdowns from a parent and being told to get his front elbow nice and high. Another has just finally grasped the LBW law. Another is leafing through her first *Wisden*. Another is wide-eyed, transfixed as he is told the story of Keith Miller by a grandparent.

Cricket will evolve; it always has. But we can invest legitimate hope in the idea that it will remain a unique sanctuary, a place of subtlety, charm, integrity and decency; and that it will always be infused with something intangible but magical, indefinable but instinctively understood by all: the spirit of cricket.

SPIRIT OF CRICKET XI

There are millions of players at all levels who have embodied the spirit of cricket, so whittling them down to a final XI is arguably pointless. Therefore, that's precisely what I've done. With a heavy heart over the exclusion of Brian Close in particular, here's my entirely unscientific selection of those who, in their very different ways, captured the beauty and spirit of cricket.

JACK HOBBS
England, Surrey (First class career: 1905–1934)

The miracle of Sir Jack Hobbs is not how many runs he scored, but how many runs he did not. His records of 61,760 runs and 199 hundreds in first-class cricket will never be broken, yet both totals – particularly the first – might have been significantly greater. The First World War cost him four years of his absolute prime, between the ages of 32 and 36. Perhaps more significantly, Hobbs was a man who did not care for statistical achievement – he deplored the publication of averages and felt the game would be better without them – and tailored his batting accordingly.

For Surrey in particular he would frequently give his wicket away upon reaching a century, feeling that he had done his job and that somebody else deserved a go. Hobbs knew the price of every run and the value of it too, which is why he so often excelled on bad wickets. 'That,' he said, 'was the time you had to earn your living.' In his debut series, against Australia, he made a startlingly authoritative 57 out of a total of 105 on a sticky dog so awkward that that other bad-wicket maestro, Victor Trumper, made a pair. 'Few men – even he – can ever have played a better bad-wicket innings,' said his teammate Jack Crawford.

Hobbs would also take the calculated risks necessary for the greater good. On turning tracks, he would often launch into a dangerous assault against the brilliant left-arm spinner Charlie Parker, hitting him out of the attack so that Parker was left grazing in the outfield when he should have been bowling on a helpful wicket.

He may have officially been a Player, but he was one of the true gentlemen of life, never mind cricket. Hobbs was a genius without any of the trappings; a thoroughly nice human being for whom barely anybody had a bad word. When giving his wicket away, he would often unobtrusively reward the man who had felt most deserved it on the opposing side. 'He would say "Well bowled" or salute you with his bat,' said Greville Stevens, 'and you felt like you had been knighted.' For all that, he remained entirely humble: he did not invite his Surrey opening partner, and hero, Tom Hayward to his wedding, feeling it was not appropriate. This gentle, shy man never got to grips with public affection.

There was so much else to admire about Hobbs, not least his inspiring technical mastery. He was simply, as his nickname stated, The Master. 'A snick by Jack Hobbs,' wrote Neville Cardus, 'is a sort of disturbance of cosmic orderliness.' His judgement of length was astonishingly good; the consequence, said his biographer John Arlott, of an 'instinctive comprehension of the bowled ball'. Then there was the way he modified his game after the war. Hobbs scored nearly 100 centuries after his 40th birthday, a startling achievement. Even that he addressed modestly, saying simply: 'I was never half the player after the first war that I was before.'

VICTOR TRUMPER
Australia, New South Wales (1894/95–1913/14)

In our eyes, Victor Trumper will be forever young. Not only because he died at 37 after contracting Bright's disease, but because of the way he played: so unfettered, with such joy, style, humility and innocence. When Arthur Mailey dismissed Trumper, he said that he 'felt like a boy who killed a dove'. As Gideon Haigh says, he simply *is* the Golden Age of cricket. 'In the gaiety and gallantry of his strokeplay, the charm of his personality, even in his frailty, transience and suddenness of death, Trumper personifies what we understand as the values and nature of his time.'

The current obsession with the Baggy Green was presaged by Trumper's love of his Australian skull cap, for which he refused to consider a replacement. He was also a hugely generous soul, who, legend has it, handed out pennies to impoverished children before a day's play during the Sydney Test to allow them to get in. His Test average is an ostensibly modest 39.04, which puts him between Basil Williams and Marvan Atapattu, yet he is the only batsman whom you could seriously compare to Don Bradman in an Australian pub without being laughed out of town.

Unlike Bradman, Trumper excelled on all wickets. In the wet English summer of 1902 he scored 2570 runs, including 11 centuries, only two fewer than the rest of the Australian squad combined. According to *Wisden*, he 'reduced our best bowlers to the level of the village green.' Trumper has a strong case for being the greatest bad-wicket player of them all. Not only could he survive on sticky dogs, but he would play the most brilliant attacking innings to reverse the momentum. He was never better than at Melbourne in 1903-04, when he lashed 74 out of a total of 122 against England as Wilfred Rhodes ran riot.

COLIN COWDREY
England, Kent (1950–1976)

Nobody embraced cricket quite like Colin Cowdrey. Nobody welcomed every facet of the game with such fascination and such an acceptant attitude towards the game's vicissitudes, however much they sapped him. 'She was a mistress never to be taken for granted,' he said of cricket. 'She gave me her richest prizes and her cruellest lessons.'

He gave her so much in return. Two particular incidents have justly entered folklore: when he walked out to bat with a broken arm against the West Indies at Lord's in 1963; and his ludicrous, jaunty meeting with Jeff

Thomson at Perth in 1974-75, when, having been flown out at short notice at the age of 42, he disarmed the fastest bowler in the world with a cheery 'Good morning, my name's Cowdrey.'

Thomson was one of the thousands whose acquaintance Cowdrey was privileged to make as a result of his time in cricket. He revelled in the social side of the game, almost always sporting that familiar ruddy, avuncular smile. Some felt he was a touch too nice and did not achieve true greatness as a consequence; if so, there are worse failings. He was also a proud Anglophile and had a cover-drive that left no brow in the house unfurrowed, the apex of a lustrous natural talent.

After his retirement, Cowdrey become cricket's great uncle, gently trying to keep his favourite nephew on the straight and narrow. The thought of cricket losing its spirit horrified him, and it was he who came up with the idea for The Spirit of Cricket to feature in the Preamble to the Laws of the Game. It was a perfect legacy for a man who cared desperately for the game and held it in his heart.

In his autobiography, he wrote that, 'If I was given a choice as my last act on earth, it would be to walk to the wicket on the lovely St. Lawrence Ground at Canterbury in the sunshine, with the pavilion chattering and the small tents buzzing. I would then lean into a half-volley just outside the off-stump, praying that the old timing still lived in the wrists to send it speeding down the slope past cover's left hand to the old tree for four.'

FRANK WORRELL
West Indies, Barbados, Jamaica (1941/4-1963/64)

Frank Worrell was cricket's great unifier; a man who, as the first black captain of the West Indies, brought together the islands in a way that had previously been thought impossible. It was appropriate that he was born in Barbados but spent most of his adult life in Trinidad and Jamaica before his tragically premature death at the age of 42. 'His greatest contribution,' said Sir Learie Constantine, 'was to destroy forever the myth that a coloured cricketer was not fit to lead a team.' His was an extraordinary influence. 'Worrell embodied all that was noble and deeply attractive in the West Indian character,' wrote Ronaldi Austin. 'Articulate, sensitive and West Indian to the core, he gave substance to the view that unity should be the hallmark of the region and its cricket team.'

Worrell's concerns went way beyond the cricket field. C. L. R. James said that he was 'possessed of an almost unbridled passion for social equality' and, such was Worrell's political influence that some are almost unaware of what a sublime player he was, a splendidly elegant batsman who averaged just shy of 50 and a very useful left-arm seamer. After a starburst of runs at the turn of the 1950s, *The Cricketer* said that 'There was no memory of anyone scoring runs in every class of cricket with such grace and power.'

In 1961-62, he saved the life of the Indian batsman Nari Contractor by donating blood when Contractor was struck horribly by a bouncer from Charlie Griffith. As a man of the rarest dignity and enormous internal strength, he set the perfect example to his team. He made walking compulsory and preached attacking cricket; that ethos, shared by Richie Benaud, produced one of the great Test series, between West Indies and Australia in 1960-61. The series could have been a 0-0 borefest and Worrell's place in history, as the man who broke down barriers and made the West Indies a recognisable team, would still have been secure.

GARRY SOBERS

West Indies, Barbados, Nottinghamshire, South Australia
(1952/53–1974)

It was apt that Sir Garfield Sobers became the first man to hit six sixes in an over in first-class cricket, for here was a man who knew only attack. He was also the definitive all-rounder: he had all the shots, bowled seam, orthodox spin or wrist spin, and fielded peerlessly in almost any position. He struck the ball with such style and power that, according to Bishan Bedi, 'Even bowling to him and being punished was a delight.' Sobers' ceaseless commitment to attacking cricket manifested itself most famously in an infamous, match-losing declaration against England in 1967-68, a decision for which he was savaged by the short-sighted. He took the abuse with dignity and class.

He was a walker. He made big hundreds at breakneck speed – he converted his first Test century into a world-record 365 not out – and, like all the true greats, he scored runs when they mattered. Perhaps his best innings came at Sabina Park against England in 1967-68. He made a golden duck in the first innings, and West Indies followed on 233 behind on a cracked pitch that was lifting and spitting horribly. Sobers proceeded to ward off defeat with a staggering, unbeaten 113. As if that wasn't enough, he then dismissed Geoff Boycott and Colin Cowdrey in the first over of the England innings. England eventually held on desperately for a draw at 68 for eight.

In addition, Sobers – an astonishing natural athlete whom Ray Robinson described as 'evolution's ultimate specimen in cricketers' – played golf, basketball and football for Barbados, a true sportsman in both senses. 'He had that rare quality, seen in a Bobby Charlton or a Gary Lineker, which allows the game to be played at the highest level without histrionics, temper or exaggerated effort,' said Ted Dexter. 'No player I have seen in my lifetime so embodies all the principles set out in the newly adopted preamble under the heading "The Spirit of Cricket".'

KEITH MILLER
Australia, New South Wales, Nottinghamshire, Victoria
(1937/38 – 1959)

This Miller had thousands of tales to tell, a reflection of a life extraordinarily well lived. A man of rare charisma and sublime talent, he was also a throughly good egg, given a life-altering perspective by his experiences in the Second World War. This prompted his most famous quote: 'I'll tell you what pressure is. Pressure is a Messerschmitt up your arse, playing cricket is not.' Miller deplored the murderous ambition of others, and famously allowed himself to be bowled first ball when Australia made a world-record 721 runs in a day against Essex in 1948. He was only interested in game-changing contributions: a sudden spell of brutish, almost pantomime short stuff to liven up a sleepy crowd and a drifting contest, or a couple of hours of unfettered hitting, both of which were amply demonstrated when lorded over the post-war Victory Tests of 1945. 'Crowd involvement is an essential part of the Miller story,' wrote his biographer Mihir Bose. 'Miller was always able to provoke a crowd; he occasionally angered them; he sometimes saddened them; he never bored them.'

Miller was happy bowling long, long spells for the cause and formed one of the great new-ball partnerships with Ray Lindwall. He was also, along with Shane Warne, one of Australia's Great Lost Captains. Richie Benaud rated him as the finest leader he ever played under. He inspired just as much awe off the field; he was impossibly charismatic and absurdly handsome, rugged but also pretty, and there were rumours of a relationship with Princess Margaret. With his shirt unbuttoned and right hand drawn magnetically through his luxuriant hair, he would hold a crowd in his thrall, effortlessly clearing bars and boundaries. He was a superstar who had the qualities of an everyman. 'Miller's influence,' said Fred Trueman, 'had to be seen to be believed.' Whether he was batting, bowling or being, you just could not take your eyes off him.

ADAM GILCHRIST
Australia, New South Wales, Western Australia
(1992/93–2007/08)

It's not only bowlers who might have just cause to dislike Gilchrist. Every single wicketkeeper in cricket history has had his career put in the most unflattering context by the emergence of a man who completely redefined the role. It had already moved from wicketkeeper to wicketkeeper-batsman but now, after Gilchrist, it will always be batsman-wicketkeeeper. His simple four-word philosophy – 'just hit the ball' – sums up an approach that has induced many a four-letter lament from bowlers. His whirring, roundhouse cut shot and whistle-clean slog-sweep are his strongest suits, but his book of shots contains no gaps, and few can match a riotous strike-rate of over 80 in Tests and just shy of 100 in ODIs. None can match his selflessness either: few players have ever put the needs of the team so far above those of the self, and nobody else has ever walked in a World Cup semi-final.

That is, not unreasonably, seen as his premier contribution to the spirit of cricket, yet almost as relevant is his ceaseless commitment to attack. His average and strike-rate would be impressive enough even if he had not played with such thrilling disregard for them. When he was on a pair against England at Brisbane in 2002-03, he hit his second ball for six, because it was the right thing to do for a team chasing a declaration. If he had got out, so be it. When he was promoted to No3 at Kandy in 2003-04, with Australia trailing and Gilchrist having scored 14 runs in his previous innings, he smashed Muttiah Muralitharan everywhere in a bravura, match-winning 144 from 185 balls. Even by his standards, it was an astonishing performance. He is the game's good Samaritan; even if you want to dislike him, you just can't.

RICHIE BENAUD
Australia, New South Wales (1948/49–1963/64)

Even had he not bowled a ball, not captained Australia with such distinction for so long, Richie Benaud would still be one of the greats of the game. It seems extraordinary that so many children ask Benaud whether he ever played the game, but that is testament to the enduring quality of his commentary. Combine the two and you have the grandfather of cricket: sagacious and profound, but still with a mischievous twinkle in his eye. He is, as Gideon Haigh says, 'cricket's most admired and pervasive post-war personality'.

Benaud's commentary has been defined by a number of things: that deadpan humour, a never-ending love of the game, particularly leg-spin, and most of all brevity. Benaud quickly grasped the lesson that less was more in commentary, and that the mouth was only to be opened if it had something to add to the pictures. When Benaud talks, you listen. He has also been superb at reacting to unexpected events. When, for example, Glenn McGrath bowled Kevin Pietersen just as Benaud was ending his final commentary on British television at The Oval in 2005, he combined the two elements seamlessly: 'It's been a great deal of fun... but not for the batsman, McGrath has picked him up.'

Benaud picked up plenty of batsmen as a legspinner of the highest class with 248 wickets at Test level. He was also a dashing lower-middle order batsman and perhaps Australia's finest captain, whose commitment to attacking cricket manifested itself most obviously in the wonderful series against the West Indies in 1960-61, which restored the game to full health after some tedious series. He never lost a series as Australian captain.

RICHARD HADLEE

New Zealand, Canterbury, Nottinghamshire, Tasmania
(1971/72-1990)

Some are born great, some achieve greatness, and some work and work and work until greatness has no choice but to thrust itself upon them. If Sir Richard Hadlee had cocooned himself in a laboratory for 20 years with the sole intention of creating the perfect fast bowler, he could hardly have done any better. Hadlee was, in cricket terms, a self-made millionaire. After a dodgy start, as he discovered his identity – he averaged 51 with the ball after five Tests and 31 after 25 – he became almost unplayable.

A tearaway in his youth, he moulded himself into a master craftsman, scientifically studying every nuance of fast bowling while honing an immaculate action. It was an action that produced bounce and extraordinary seam movement when there was no right to expect any, particularly in a snarling leg-cutter that terrorised right-handers.

He bore a burden like no other player – at least until the emergence of Muttiah Muralitharan – but those upright shoulders never showed any sign of surrender. Some might say it's easy to play for the team when you basically *are* the team, but that belittles Hadlee's sportsmanlike nature. When he took a superb catch to deny himself a ten-wicket haul against Australia at Brisbane in 1985-86, Frank Keating called it 'the catch of the century.'

Hadlee lifted New Zealand from being little more than a punching bag to a team that would not lose a series at home, not even to the great West Indies side, in the 1980s. His work with the new ball was always immaculate and intensely probing, and he usually saved his best for Australia. He was quiet and humble, often barely bothering to celebrate wickets. This, after all, was his job. He was also stunningly reliable; in his 17 last Test series he never averaged as much as 27. In contrast with his bowling, his lower-order biffing was rather less scientific, but when it came off it was often explosive and game-changing.

BISHAN BEDI
India, Delhi, Northamptonshire, Northern Punjab
(1961/62–1980/81)

Those who would suggest that a comparison between art and cricket is fatuous have obviously never seen Bishan Bedi. His left-arm spin was a joy to behold, both in his unimaginably pure action and in his spellbinding variety. Bedi was a master of deception, who mixed his flight, dip, pace and spin with no discernible change in action. A Bedi delivery was as seductive as a *femme fatale*, and every bit as deadly. And it was all delivered with a smile and a quip from under his signature bright patka.

'A few easy rhythmic steps, perfectly balanced, and he moved smoothly into the delivery stride,' said Mike Brearley. 'There was no sense of striving, nothing rushed or snatched, no hiccoughs, just an easy flow. He bowled at the slower end of the spin bowler's range, though not dead slow.' There is a stunning picture of Bedi, taken in 1974 by Ken Kelly, who followed him around for four years to capture it. Bedi is just about to deliver the ball, and his right hand has come all the way over to the top of his head so that his right thumb is touching the top of the ball, pushing it further into the grip of his left hand. It was, said Kelly, 'an amazing final unconscious check to establish that his purchase on the ball was exactly perfect.' Bedi did not even realise he was doing it.

He was part of one of the game's great brotherhoods, the Indian spin quartet that also included Bhagwat Chandrasekhar, Erapalli Prasanna and Srinivas Venkataraghavan. And he had a novel approach to training those long fingers to rip the ball: he kept them strong and supple by washing all his own clothes.

Bedi has become known for some extremely strong criticism of the likes of Muttiah Muralitharan, yet even that is born of concern for the game and a sincere belief that Muralitharan is a chucker. Out in the middle he was an extremely generous soul, who would sincerely applaud batsmen if they were good enough to hit him for six.

Bedi was always a man of deeply-held convictions. He effectively declared India's innings at five wickets down against West Indies at Sabina Park in 1975-76, a response to tyrannical fast bowling. He also conceded a one-day international against Pakistan in 1978-79, even though India were cruising to victory, when the umpires failed to wide Sarfraz Nawaz for a series of bouncers. 'I was embroiled in many controversies,' he said, 'because I couldn't stand foul play.'

BRIAN STATHAM
England, Lancashire (1950–1968)

The myth that a fast bowler must have a nasty streak to be successful was shattered by Brian Statham. Although he picked up 2260 first-class wickets at the astonoshing average of 16.37, Statham 'bowled without a trace of animosity' according to Peter May, and would go so far as to warn batsmen in advance if he was to bowl a bouncer. His *Wisden* obituary said he 'was one of the best of all English fast bowlers, and beyond question the best-liked.' Statham was an, ordinary humble man who just happened to be a great fast bowler. He was self-effacement incarnate, allowing Fred Trueman and Frank Tyson to hog the limelight as he uncomplainingly bowled marathon spells into the wind; a thoroughbred who never thought he was too good to do the donkey work. 'It never mattered what you asked him to do, whether it was to come on for a few overs, to bowl until lunch, to bowl uphill or upwind,' said May. 'Whatever it was, he would take the ball and do it.'

There was not a hint of envy, even though Statham was every bit as deserving of acclaim as any bowler of his age. Few fast bowlers have been so indefatigable. If Statham lost his temper, be it with batsmen, umpires or fate, it was so rare as to be almost a JFK moment. 'Never have I seen the equanimity of Statham's temperament or technique rendered out of harmony for a minute,' wrote Neville Cardus. He was metronomic before cricket writers used the word, bowling with such devastating accuracy that he surely took many wickets at the other end as batsmen gulped desperately for the oxygen of runs that were denied them when Statham was bowling. 'If they miss, I'll hit' was his modus operandi, and Staham's approach carried something that gets to the essence of the spirit of cricket but which has been almost forgotten in recent times: bowling at the stumps.

BIBLIOGRAPHY

Jack Hobbs: Profile of the Master John Arlott (John Murray, 1981)
Opening Up: My Autobiography Mike Atherton (Coronet, 2002)
Sir Gary: A Biography Trevor Bailey (William Collins, 1976)
My Spin on Cricket Richie Benaud (Hodder & Stoughton, 2004)
"What are the Butchers For?": And Other Splendid Cricket Quotations Lawrence Booth ed. (A
    & C Black, 2009)
Keith Miller: A Cricketing Biography Mihir Bose (Allen & Unwin, 1980)
My Autobiography: Don't Tell Kath… Ian Botham (Collins Willow, 1994)
The Art of Captaincy Mike Brearley (Hodder & Stoughton, 1985)
Stiff Upper Lips and Baggy Green Caps Simon Briggs (Quercus, 2007)
I Don't Bruise Easily Brian Close (Macdonald and Jane's, 1978)
M.C.C. The Autobiography of a Cricketer Colin Cowdrey (Hodder & Stoughton, 1976)
Time to Declare Basil D'Oliveira (Star, 1982)
White Lightning Allan Donald (HarperCollinsWillow, 1999)
Behind The Shades: The Autobiography Duncan Fletcher (Simon & Schuster, 2007)
Being Freddie: My Story So Far Andrew Flintoff (Hodder & Stoughton, 2005)
Thommo David Frith (Angus and Robertson, 1980)
True Colours: My Life Adam Gilchrist (Macmillan, 2009)
Forgotten Heroes: The 1945 Australian Services Cricket Team Ed Jaggard (Sporting Traditions,
    1996)
Harold Larwood Duncan Hamilton (Quercus, 2009)
Cricket War Gideon Haigh (Text, 1993)
Jim Laker: A Biography Alan Hill (Andre Deutsch, 2002)
My Life Story John Berry Hobbs (The Star Publications, 1935)
Beyond a Boundary CLR James (Stanley Paul & Co., 1963)
The Larwood Story Harold Larwood (WH Allen, 1965)
Menace: The Autobiography Dennis Lillee (Headline, 2003)

Ten for Sixty-Six and All That Arthur Mailey (Phoenix House, 1959)

Assault On The Ashes Christopher Martin-Jenkins (Readers Union, 1975)

Lord's Geoffrey Moorhouse (Hodder & Stoughton, 1983)

The Best Loved Game Geoffrey Moorhouse (Hodder & Stoughton, 1979)

Basil D'Oliveira: Cricket and Controversy Peter Oborne (Sphere, 2005)

Viv Richards Viv Richards and David Foot (World's Work, 1979)

What Sport Tells Us About Life Ed Smith (Viking, 2008)

Quest For Number One Robin Smith (Boxtree, 1993)

Grovel! The Story and Legacy of the Summer of 1976 David Tossell (Know the Score, 2007)

Cricket's Strangest Matches Andrew Ward (Robson Books, 1999)

Ashes Diary 2001 Steve Waugh (HarperCollins, 2001)

Out of My Comfort Zone: The Autobiography Steve Waugh (Michael Joseph, 2006)

Starting With Grace: A Pictorial Celebration of Cricket 1864-1986 Bob Willis and Patrick Murphy, (Book Club Associates, 1986)

Flying Stumps and Metal Bats Wisden Cricketer (Aurum, 2008)

Various newspapers and websites, including:

Cricinfo.com

The Daily Telegraph

The Independent

The Guardian

The Times

Various periodicals, including:

The Cricketer

The Wisden Cricketer

Wisden Cricketers' Almanack

Wisden Cricket Monthly